A Brief Guide To

The History of Southwell

'The Jewel in Nottinghamshire's Crown'

Edited by

J Michael Wilkinson

Southwell and District Local History Society
2017

First published in Great Britain by
Southwell and District Local History Society

http://www.southwellhistorysociety.co.uk

ISBN 978-0-9932442-4-7

© Southwell and District Local History Society, 2017

All rights reserved. No part of this publication may be reproduced, stored or introduced into a retrieval system or transmitted in any form, by any means (electronic, mechanical, photocopy, recording or otherwise) without the prior permission of the publishers.

Whilst every care has been taken to ensure the accuracy of the information contained in this publication, Southwell and District Local History Society cannot accept any responsibility or liability for any errors or omissions.

Printed in England by Russell Press, Russell House, Bulwell Lane, Basford, Nottingham, NG6 0BT.

Contents

		Page
Contributors		iv
Illustrations		v
Map of Southwell, 2017		viii
Preface		ix
Chapter 1	Southwell Through the Ages: *Michael J Kirton*	1
Chapter 2	Roman and Saxon Southwell: *Matthew Beresford*	7
Chapter 3	The Minster and Archbishop's Palace: *Charles Leggatt*	15
Chapter 4	The Minster School: *David Hutchison*	27
Chapter 5	The Prebendal Houses: *Susan Summers*	39
Chapter 6	The Methodist, Baptist and Holy Trinity Churches: *Stanley Chapman*	49
Chapter 7	The Burgage: *Ellis Morgan*	59
Chapter 8	The Nottinghamshire House of Correction: *Robert Smith*	67
Chapter 9	The Workhouse: *Victoria Preece*	77
Chapter 10	Southwell's Inns and Alehouses: *Roger Dobson*	87
Chapter 11	Southwell's Industries: *Peter Lyth*	99
Chapter 12	In and Around the Town: *Michael J Kirton*	111

Publications by Southwell and District Local History Society   123
Index of people   125
General Index   127

Contributors

Matthew Beresford is an archaeologist with a special interest in crowd-funded community projects.

Stanley Chapman is an Emeritus Professor in the University of Nottingham International Business History Institute and is President of Southwell and District Local History Society.

Roger Dobson is a former history teacher and Deputy Head Teacher at a Nottingham comprehensive school. He is author of several publications on aspects of Southwell's history.

David Hutchison was Head of the History Department at Southwell Minster School from 1975 to 2007.

Michael Kirton is a former banker turned historian with a special interest in local Georgian history. He is Chairman of Southwell and District Local History Society.

Charles Leggatt has worked at Christie's, the London art auctioneers, as a Director of Development at Dulwich Picture Gallery and as Director of Fundraising for Southwell Minster. He coordinated the project to restore and update the Archbishop's Palace.

Peter Lyth was a University Teacher in Tourism at the Nottingham University Business School with a special interest in transport history.

Ellis Morgan is a former consultant thoracic surgeon now involved in dissecting the archaeology of Southwell and the surrounding district. He is leader of Southwell Archaeology's project: 'The Burgage Manor Revealed'.

Victoria Preece is a volunteer guide at Southwell Workhouse and a former Secretary of Southwell and District Local History Society.

Robert Smith is an accountant at Rainbow Night Freight Ltd, Newark-on-Trent. His historical interests include the House of Correction and the Southwell Settlers.

Susan Summers is Secretary of Southwell Civic Society and former Chairman of Nottinghamshire Building Preservation Trust.

Illustrations

Map of Southwell and places of interest	viii
The South Well	2
Map of Southwell town centre, 1781	4
Becher, The Revd John Thomas	6
Map of the Roman villa site	8
Roman villa plunge bath	9
Roman villa mosaic floor	10
Pottery sherds, two images	11
Roman villa burial site	12
Southwell Minster, the Norman nave	16
Southwell Minster font	17
Medieval tympanum	17
Chapter House entrance	18
Leaves of Southwell, two images	19
Chapter House carvings, two images	19
Carved mouse in Southwell Minster	19
Minster Quire and High Altar	20
Carved misericord, Minster Quire	20
First World War memorial window, Southwell Minster	21
Roman mosaic flooring, Minster south transept	22
Minster Quire and organ	22
Remains of the Archbishop of York's Palace	24
The surviving part of the Archbishop's Palace	24
The State Chamber	25
The Residence in Vicars' Court	26
Minster School early location	27
The Chantry Priests' House	28
Magnus Jackson, Minster School Headmaster 1788-1809	28
Minster Chambers, former Grammar School building	29
Minster Grammar School photograph, late 19th century	30
Minster Grammar School photograph circa 1914	31
National School, Nottingham Road, Southwell circa 1920	34

National School 'Annual Treat Day' parade, circa 1910	34
Edward Cludd School	35
Edward Cludd pupils boarding train, 1976	36
Stephen Pulford, Headmaster, Minster Grammar School and prefects, 1976	36
Part of the present Minster School	37
Sacrista Prebend	40
Map of Prebendal Houses	41
Normanton Prebend	43
Woodborough Prebend	44
Cranfield House, formerly Oxton 1 Prebend	45
Rampton Prebend	47
William Neepe's house	50
Southwell Methodist Church	51
Former Wesleyan Day School	53
Advertisement - Laying the First Stone of Holy Trinity Church	57
Holy Trinity Church	58
Burgage Green	59
Funfair on the Burgage, early 20th century	60
Burgage Manor	62
Burgage Manor, sketch by Elizabeth Pigot	63
Elmfield House, two images	66
House of Correction, 1780s plan	68
Digital reconstruction of the New House of Correction	69
House of Correction Gatehouse, architect's sketch	70
Treadwheel at Pentonville Prison	73
Cell door	74
House of Correction Gatehouse, modern photograph	76
Nottingham Road Workhouse, now the Baptist Church	77
Southwell Workhouse	78
Plan of the Workhouse	80
Money for old rope - oakum	81
A dining table at the Workhouse	81
Women's work yard at the Workhouse	83
Bedroom for the homeless at the Workhouse, 1970s	85
Map of Inns and Alehouses, and 19th century Malt Houses	88

Southwell Cocking, advertisement	90
Coaches outside the Saracen's Head Hotel	91
Wall painting, Saracen's Head Hotel, 15th century	92
Victory Parade, 1919	93
Robert Morvinson, 1857	96
Maythorne Mill	100
House of Correction, early 20th century	102
The Malthouse, Kirklington Road, Southwell	103
Ideal Cinema	104
The railway crossing, Station Road, early 20th century	105
The railway crossing, Station Road, modern image	105
Caudwell's Mill, 1930s	108
Caudwell's Mill as apartments	108
Brackenhurst Hall	109
Assembly Rooms	111
War Memorial dedication, 1921	113
Alfred Loughton	115
George Bernard Shaw	115
Easthorpe	116
The original Bramley apple tree	117
Westhorpe	119
Sunnyside Terrace, Westhorpe	120
Field Marshall Viscount Allenby	120
Westhorpe Hall	121
Southwell Racecourse	122

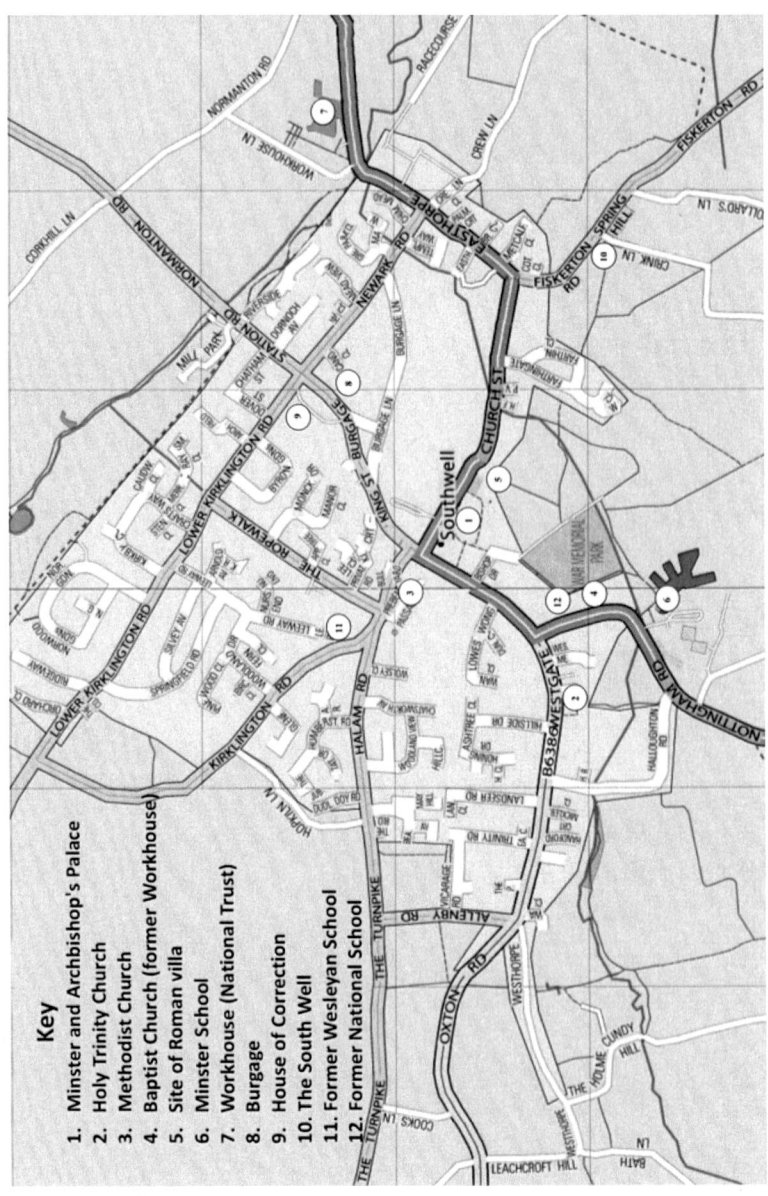

*Map of Southwell showing main places of interest -
for maps of the Prebendal Houses and Inns and Alehouses
see Chapters 5 and 10.*

Preface

The History of Southwell has been produced by Southwell and District Local History Society as an account of the main historical features of the town. The book is an attempt to satisfy the curiosity of residents and visitors who may wonder why a small town outside the major road, rail and canal networks, with neither surviving local industry other than agriculture, nor significant commerce other than a few shops, has its very own splendid medieval cathedral surrounded by magnificent Georgian houses, an Archbishop's Palace and a fully-preserved Victorian workhouse.

Pronunciation of the town's name often causes confusion because it is pronounced either as 'South-well' or as 'Suthell' (phonetic: Sŭdhl). Both pronunciations are correct. The town is described on the 'Visit Southwell' website (http://www.visitsouthwell.com) as a picturesque town, bursting with tradition and character, often referred to as *'The Jewel in Nottinghamshire's Crown'*.

The main focus of *The History of Southwell* is on the many historic buildings to see around the town, shown on the various maps. The Minster clearly dominates the town's buildings. Daniel Defoe, in his book *A Tour Through The Whole Island of Great Britain* (Vol. 3, 1727), describes his visit to Southwell: *'From hence I was going to Rugford* [Rufford] *Abbey, the fine seat of the late Marquis of Hallifax, but was called aside to take a view of the most famous piece of church history in this part of the whole island, I mean the collegiate church of Southwell'*. As you walk around the town, look out also for the blue plaques that provide brief details of several other notable places.

Southwell and District Local History Society, in addition to holding monthly meetings and visits to local places of historic interest, has produced many local history books since its establishment in 1983. A list of the Society's publications including detailed accounts of the town in two world wars, can be found on page 123.

Please visit the Society's website at:
www.southwellhistorysociety.co.uk

Southwell residents are fortunate to be surrounded by rich history and here we have tried to share the main elements of that history with you. We hope you enjoy reading *The History of Southwell* and exploring the town.

Our grateful thanks go to our contributors for their enthusiastic, thoughtful, and scholarly participation in this project.

J M Wilkinson
Editor

M J Kirton
Chairman, Southwell and District Local History Society
May 2017

Chapter 1

Southwell Through the Ages

Michael J Kirton

Southwell's origins are linked to water and roads. Early settlers probably arrived via the River Trent, the Fosse Way and the Great North Road, which are only a few miles away. They discovered that the River Greet, which runs along the northern edge of the town, its subsidiary streams and four wells, provided a reliable supply of water. In medieval times the water was believed to have healing powers. Today, as travellers approach, particularly from Thurgarton, they cannot fail to be captivated by the sight of Southwell Minster's twin 'pepper pots' dominating this small town. Weary pilgrims over hundreds of years must have felt even more impressed, if not overawed, by this magnificent place of worship which justifies Southwell being described as 'The Jewel in Nottinghamshire's Crown'. A view that is confirmed by the many Georgian buildings on the approach to the historic core of the town, culminating in the imposing prebendal houses that overlook their mother church. However, the recorded history of Southwell goes back to the Roman Empire.

Adjacent to the Minster is the site of an impressive Roman villa, probably the grandest in the area. Archaeological excavations have revealed the size of the villa, and further detailed work has shown the extent of the Roman site, including a monumental wall and a subsequent Saxon settlement. Chapter 2 reveals more. On display in the south Quire of the Minster are the remains of the ceiling of the bath house, depicting Cupid (pictured on the back cover of this book), and in the south transept are fragments of a Roman mosaic floor that can be inspected through a glass plate in one of the pews. This may be from an earlier church as evidence suggests that the Minster was built around it.

An early Roman visitor to the town is said to be Paulinus, Archbishop of York, who dedicated his life to converting the north of England to

Christianity. In AD 625, on his journey north from Canterbury, he stopped in Southwell to baptise converts; the location is marked by a small monument to the 'South Well' on the road to Fiskerton.

*Plaque marking the site of the 'South Well', at the junction of Fiskerton Road and Crink Lane.
(Mike Kirton)*

Little is known of the following years until AD 956 when records show that Archbishop Oskytel was granted the manor, and the estate was doubled to around 20,000 acres after the Norman Conquest. Southwell became a convenient staging post on the archbishops' journeys from York to Canterbury. The building of the Minster commenced in 1108, with completion by 1300. In the 1360s (altered in the 1500s) a large manor house, the Archbishop's Palace, was built alongside the Norman collegiate church (see Chapter 3). Only parts of the palace have survived, but the extent of the house can be seen from the ruins of the remainder, which have been preserved with the help of Lottery funding. The intact State Chamber has been renovated and is well worth a visit. It is in use for functions and exhibitions. By the side of the palace, and adjacent to the Archbishop's deer park, an educational garden has been created and is a peaceful escape from the town. Across the deer park, now used for recreational purposes, there are extensive views of the surrounding countryside.

Before it became a cathedral in 1884 the Minster was a collegiate church run by a chapter of canons, who derived their income from several communities within the Peculiar[1] of Southwell. These villages are recorded in the names of the impressive prebendal houses, which are described in more detail in Chapter 5. For over a thousand years Southwell Minster's chapter of canons was the administrative centre for a large part of Nottinghamshire. It was the religious body responsible for the running of the Minster and its estates on behalf of the archbishops of York who were the Lords of the Manor. In addition, the chapter also administered church courts, separate to the archbishop's jurisdiction, which sat in various locations around Nottinghamshire so that local people did not have far to travel to attend the sessions. The chapter was responsible for granting marriage licences to, and proving the wills of, people who lived in 28 local rural parishes. The Peculiar also created employment for non-cleric professionals. We know that in the 18th century successive County Coroners were appointed from the ranks of local attorneys (lawyers). Other attorneys acted as Registrars to the Minster Chapter, undertaking varying professional duties, until powers eventually passed to Southwell Rural District Council, which existed until 1974 when local government was passed to Newark and Sherwood District Council.

As well as assisting the chapter with administration, local lawyers had also been involved in administering the Leadenham - Mansfield and Southwell - Oxton Turnpike. At the onset of the Industrial Revolution this was an important route for carting coal from Mansfield to the east coast ports. The demise of the turnpikes came with the building of canals and the development of the railways.

In recent years the very active Southwell Community Archaeology Group has discovered evidence of a medieval settlement on the Burgage

---

[1] A Peculiar jurisdiction was a parish or a number of parishes exempt from the jurisdiction of the bishop of the diocese.

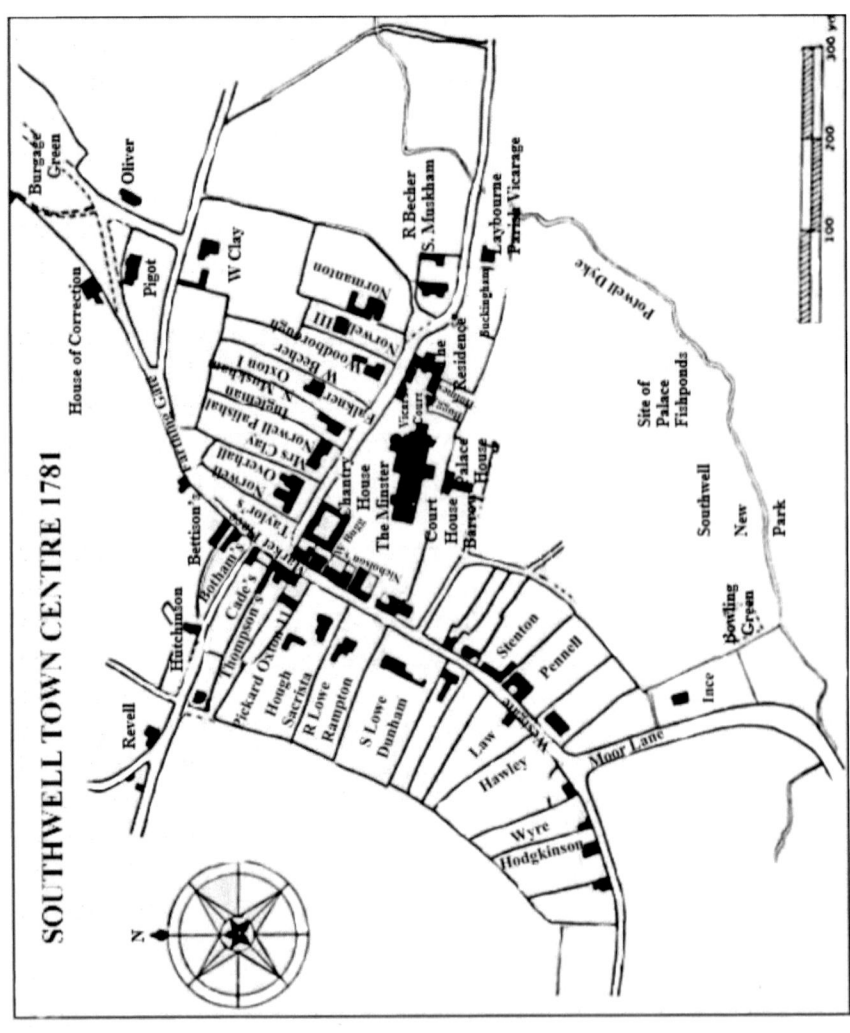

The above map shows the location of many of the influential Georgians. It is interesting to note that the basic layout of the town centre has not changed in hundreds of years. In the 18th century most people lived close to the Minster. Normanton, Easthorpe and Westhorpe were separate communities.

(Adapted from 'Georgian Southwell', Hardstaff and Lyth, 1986)

and investigations are ongoing. This area of the town was the site of the former Nottinghamshire House of Correction (Chapter 8). It is reasonable to ask why Southwell should have the county's House of Correction? The answer lies in the former importance of Southwell as an administrative centre.

Nottinghamshire experienced many Civil War skirmishes due to the sieges of royalist Newark. Parliamentarian forces were billeted in the Minster and in the already decaying Palace, which was badly damaged. One notable event during the conflict was the surrender of Charles I to the Scots at Kelham on 5th May 1646, having spent his last hours of freedom at Southwell's historic Saracen's Head Hotel (see Chapter 10).

Southwell has not been noted for industry, other than agriculture, but there was an element of framework knitting, spinning and weaving from the late 17th century (Chapter 11). In common with the country as a whole, many people scratched a living from the land, however, by the 18th century the Enclosure Acts heralded the modernisation of farming with the growth of larger holdings. One of these larger estates was centred on Norwood Park, farmed by the Sutton family on copyhold land belonging to the church. In the latter half of the 18th century it was owned by Sir Richard Sutton, a senior member of Lord North's administration. During this period the estate was managed by a local steward, George Hodgkinson (and later his son), who recorded in his diaries that hops were grown. The name lives on in Hopkiln Lane, off the Halam Road. As small tenant farming became unprofitable, many left the land and joined new industries, with some moving to the coal mines of Nottinghamshire.

In the late 19th century, following the closure of the House of Correction, lace making came to the town, occupying the substantial buildings, and by the early 20th century Careys of Nottingham were the largest employers with 150 people, most of them highly skilled. Many of the younger male employees were members of the local territorial army (1st/8th Battalion, Sherwood Foresters) and were early recruits to the trenches of the First World War, with as many as 60 serving their country. Earlier, in the 18th and 19th centuries, some of the wealthy secular families, who had served the church in various capacities, built their own prestigious houses in the town in the areas of the Burgage,

Burgage Lane and Westhorpe - mostly between 1780 and 1820 (see Chapter 7). At this time the town became a fashionable location, and from 1803 to 1808 the young Lord Byron and his mother rented the newly built Burgage Manor. Some of the families subscribed to the Assembly Rooms where they enjoyed formal dances and other genteel amusements, such as card games. The building has subsequently been incorporated into the Saracen's Head Hotel - a blue plaque on Westgate provides some detail. One notable family that settled in Southwell was the Bechers, who had their roots in Ireland. The most well-known member being the Revd John Thomas Becher (1770-1848). He was Vicar-General of the Minster and a local Justice of the Peace. Becher had influence over the design and running of the second House of Correction to be built in Southwell and also the building of the Workhouse, and was very much involved in influencing the drafting of the Poor Laws with the aim of reducing the cost of poor relief (see Chapter 9). His great-grandson John, a lawyer, led the local territorial army company in the First World war and tragically lost his life as a result of wounds received in late 1915. Sadly his son, also John, was killed serving in the RAF in 1940 and is buried in Aden.

Revd John Thomas Becher. (National Trust)

Southwell's lack of industrial growth meant that over many years the population only grew modestly, in 1801 it is recorded at 2,300 and for the first half of the 20th century it hovered around 3,500. However, with the growth of motor car ownership, Southwell became a convenient place for commuting to Nottingham and Mansfield, creating a spurt of housing development, which continues, and the population of the town is now in excess of 7,200. Today, with a choice of road and rail links, the town is home to people who commute to work in many towns and cities, including London. Young families are attracted to Southwell by its good schools, especially the Minster School that has its roots in the town's early history (Chapter 4). Southwell is still a relatively 'genteel' place and very much a tourist attraction.

Chapter 2

Roman and Saxon Southwell

Matthew Beresford

Tracing the early occupation of Southwell and its foundations as a settlement is not an easy task as pre-Roman evidence is slight. In the Roman period (AD 43 to 410), the town had a 'villa' structure that would have dominated the landscape, and a large cemetery and related church were built close to the villa site in the subsequent Saxon period (AD 410 to 1066). In the 10th century, Bishop Oskytel granted a Charter for the foundation of the Minster, and a substantial Archbishop's Palace was constructed to the side of the church (Chapter 3).

Little is known, however, of how and why the villa was built here, or indeed of any settlement at Southwell before the Roman period. A few isolated finds of prehistoric flint tools have been made in a couple of gardens on Lower Kirklington Road, close to the junction with the Burgage, and two or three basic flint tools were found during test-pitting on the Burgage Green itself in 2013. These sites are all quite close to the River Greet, so this may have been the focus of early occupation in the town.

An Iron Age coin (a gold 'stater') was found many years ago on the Brackenhurst ridge above the Farthingate area, and the early antiquarian William Dickinson sketched some bank and ditch earthworks in the town that he believed may have been part of an early defensive structure, although subsequent development has pretty much removed all trace of these today. Apart from these chance finds it was not until the villa was constructed, probably in the late 2nd century, that Southwell appeared on the map.

It should come as no surprise that some form of early settlement existed at Southwell. The Roman military advancement northwards in the 1st century saw forts constructed a mile or two to the south (Ad Pontem at East Stoke) and to the north (Osmanthorpe at Kirklington).

Southwell itself sits exactly halfway between the two, and a Roman road system linked all three sites, passing along the bottom of what is today the Burgage Green (Lower Kirklington Road).

Recent research by the Roman Southwell Community Project has shown that some form of occupation existed on the villa site in the 1st century prior to the construction of the villa itself. Pits and drainage gullies have also been found on the land adjacent to the villa site on Church Street (the site of the old Minster School and now a public open space under the custodianship of Southwell Minster), and 1st century pottery has been recovered from a garden on Farthingate. Clearly, some form of occupation existed here prior to the construction of the stone-built villa. It is hoped more fieldwork and research will help shed light on what this early occupation looked like.

In the mid-late 2nd century, stone buildings with mosaic floors were built in the area between what is today the old school site and the Minster. The stone buildings have long gone, but traces have been found in the gardens of Vicars' Court, the Residence and in the Orchard (see map). Antiquarian records suggest these wall foundations and mosaic

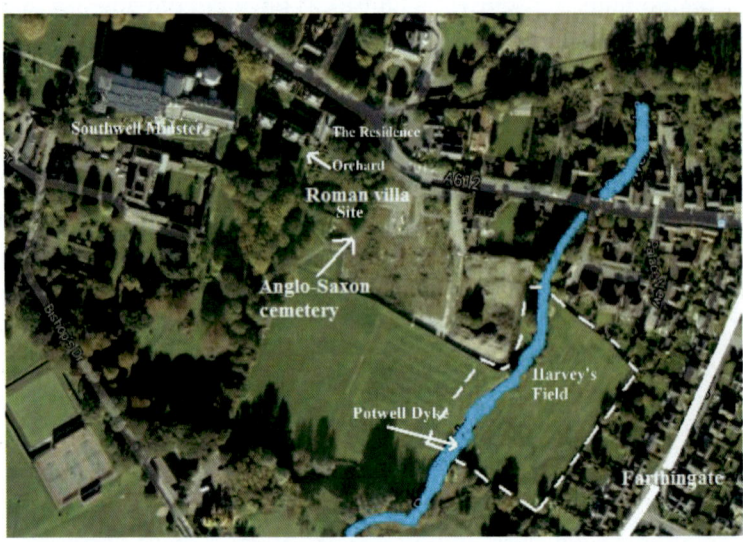

Map of Roman villa and sites of archaeological interest close to the Minster. The dotted white line indicates the area of recent investigation. (Matthew Beresford)

*Southwell Roman villa plunge bath with painted plaster.
(By kind permission of the University of Nottingham Archaeology Museum)*

floors were 1.5 to 1.8 metres below modern ground level in the area closest to the Minster.

At some point over the next few decades, it seems at least one of these buildings was demolished and a new one constructed on a slightly different alignment. This new building contained a bath house with painted wall plaster. Then, in another phase of redevelopment, the bath was demolished - the wall plaster was pulled off and dumped in the bottom of the bath, and rubble was used to fill it in. Finally, a new mortar floor was laid, sealing the bath until its discovery in the 1950s. Some of the wall plaster has an image of Cupid, or a water nymph, and can be seen on display on the south wall of the Minster

New mosaic floors were laid out in the villa buildings, and these have been dated to the 4th century based on their form and style. The designs are markedly similar to those of the Mansfield Woodhouse Roman villa, just a few miles to the north-west, perhaps suggesting some link between the two. This must have been the villa's heyday and, from the parts of it that have been rediscovered, a ground plan suggests an East Wing just to the east of the Residence, and a South Wing in the Orchard area. Wall foundations were found in 2003 on the opposite side of Church Street, under the triangular shaped open space abutting South Muskham Prebend. Contemporary floor deposits and pottery place this

*Mosaic floor in the south wing of the Roman villa at Southwell.
(By kind permission of the University of Nottingham Archaeology Museum)*

in the 1st to 2nd centuries, so although it is often suggested to be the villa's North Wing, it appears too early for this. It almost certainly formed part of those original buildings that were demolished to make way for the later, larger villa. No other Roman archaeology was known of anywhere else in the town, except for the odd coin or piece of pottery, until recently.

Excavations on the land known as Harvey's Field, adjacent to the villa site, in 2014 and 2015 by the Roman Southwell Community Project uncovered undisturbed Roman layers that suggested the whole area had flooded on a number of occasions, from at least Roman times to the present day. Several pieces of Roman pottery were recovered from these undisturbed layers, and two separate sections of a narrow ditch feature were uncovered. This ditch continued at least one metre under the present ground surface, where the water table was reached. Crucially, a single piece of Roman pottery was recovered from each of the two sections, and these were lying towards the bottom of the ditch. They were also on the same alignment as ditches and gullies discovered in excavations on the old school site, and were deemed to be 1st to 2nd century.

Roman pot sherds recently discovered in Harvey's Field, Southwell. (Matthew Beresford)

The ditches were most likely part of a Roman drainage system, built to help drain water from the floodplain of the river (now known as the Potwell Dyke). This may well hint that there was indeed a civilian settlement in this region, possibly on Farthingate as this area sits slightly higher up in the landscape. Fieldwork in 2016 revealed an abundance of Roman pottery in several gardens along Farthingate, and an undisturbed Roman rubble dump was uncovered that was full of building material, floor and roof tiles, and dozens of sherds of Roman pottery, including repaired Samian ware (1st / 2nd century) and part of a colander. Excavations on Harvey's Field showed that flooding had occurred at least sixty-five metres away from the river itself, and the villa sat within this landscape. That seems an odd place to build a villa, but considering that a large Saxon cemetery and the subsequent Minster were built in exactly this same landscape, perhaps there was something special, spiritual even, about this region all the way back in Roman times, and possibly earlier.

We do not yet know the villa's purpose. The term 'villa' is rather vague, and these types of buildings served different purposes in the

Roman period. Although there were different types of villa structure, Southwell appears to have been a courtyard villa, with buildings set around an inner courtyard. Generally, villas were farmsteads, albeit often quite grandiose, part of an estate that usually comprised other associated buildings, farm land and sometimes their own burial site or a family mausoleum. Other villa structures served as administrative centres, country retreats or, occasionally, held a religious function. Some of these villas, for example Chedworth in Gloucestershire, contained pagan shrines linked to water gods. Which of these functions the villa at Southwell performed we do not know.

Nor do we know when the villa at Southwell was eventually abandoned, but the evidence nationally is generally sometime in the late 4th century. The Roman military were pulled out of Britain in AD 410, and the country was left to fend for itself. Excavations in the 1950s and again in the 2000s identified a number of skeletons in the general area where the villa was located, and a couple of these have been dated to the mid-late 8th century, suggesting the villa had gone by this point. Many of the grave cuts had been dug down onto the mosaic floor, and several skeletons were found laid out on top of the mosaics, again suggesting the villa had gone by then. However, this still leaves a gap of around 350 years. Without more information, and more accurate dating, we will never know exactly when the villa at Southwell was abandoned.

Burials in the south wing of the Roman villa.
(By kind permission of the University of Nottingham Archaeology Museum)

Although some of the Saxon cemetery was identified through excavations, the largest number of burials was found in the early 1960s, when building work in preparation for new school buildings revealed almost 250 skeletons. Unfortunately, these were not fully recorded or properly excavated, and the archaeologist in charge of recording them only had time to draw a plan of the burials before they were removed from the site. Nevertheless, he was able to ascertain a general view of the cemetery, and suggested some of the burials seemed to be in family plots. Almost 300 burials are now known for the Saxon cemetery at Southwell, and this is a vast number for the period, far too many to be the deceased from Southwell alone. It therefore appears that people were coming to Southwell from afar in the Saxon period. There would be no reason to transport the deceased to Southwell for burial as laws at the time stated the deceased were to be buried in their home parish. For this not to happen, and for them to be buried at Southwell instead, meant that people were effectively paying twice, once to their home parish, and again to Southwell. It is more likely that people who were ill were travelling to Southwell for some reason, in the hope that they could find salvation here. Given the town's name - the South Well - it is tempting to link this salvation with water. This may not be as speculative as it first appears. We know that the villa, the Saxon cemetery (and church, we could assume) and the Minster were all built in an area that flooded. The villa had links to water through its bath house with its decorations on a water theme, and the Minster itself was built directly on top of natural underground springs. Perhaps it was believed that Southwell's water had healing properties, which was why a great number of people travelled here in the Saxon period, and why one of the largest Roman villas in the East Midlands and the Minster itself were both built here.

This large cemetery needed a church and at present there are two suggestions as to where this was located. The first and most widely accepted place is directly under the Minster. Roman mosaic floors can still be seen under the floor of the south transept of the Minster, and due to the irregularity of the individual mosaic tiles or tesserae it is argued that it is not in fact of Roman date, but rather re-laid from the villa as part of the original Saxon church floor. Although this is indeed possible, it is not a widely known practice for the Saxons to do this, and very few other examples of this have been found. There is no reason why the floor might not be a preserved Roman floor, part of an early building linked to the villa, or in fact part of the villa.

The second option, and the more likely given the location of the Saxon cemetery, is that the original church was further to the east, somewhere in the region of the Residence or South Muskham Prebend. Interestingly, part of an early wall can be noted built into the boundary wall to the rear of South Muskham Prebend next to the public footpath. This could easily be part of an early church, and is in the right location if the second option is correct.

That there was such a large cemetery at Southwell in the Saxon period suggests there was a wider settlement here, although like its Roman predecessor it is proving difficult to trace. Bank and ditch earthworks running along the eastern boundary of Edgehill House (from Burgage Back Lane down to Church Street) have been suggested as Saxon. Excavations by the University of Nottingham located the ditch for these earthworks, the fill of which contained a metal pin of Saxon date. Similarly, curious banked earthworks have been noted running from the entrance to Lowes Wong school on Halam Road in a south-westerly direction right across to Lowes Wong. These, and the Edgehill earthworks, have been proposed by the University as being part of a Saxon defensive 'burh'. Burhs were first constructed in the late 9th century by Alfred the Great in order to defend England from continued Viking attacks. However, this theory is far from accepted, and the Edgehill earthworks appear to curve eastwards at the top, and not westwards towards those at Lowes Wong. Much like the possible defensive structure proposed by Dickinson (and mentioned earlier), it seems more likely that these two sets of earthworks are not related and are rather part of two entirely separate features. Their exact purpose sadly remains unclear.

The overall picture for Roman and Saxon Southwell is a partial one. We have tantalising glimpses into this early part of the town's history, and features such as the Roman villa and large-scale Saxon cemetery are enigmatic, yet are far from the full picture. Each time new research and fieldwork are undertaken we gain a few more pieces of the puzzle. In fact, we could say that the situation is like a giant jigsaw puzzle where half of the pieces are missing! Nevertheless, the parts we do know are fascinating and suggest a rich historical tapestry for Southwell, one that becomes richer still as we progress into the Medieval period.

Chapter 3

Southwell Minster and the Archbishop's Palace

Charles Leggatt

The Minster

From 19th century journals to *Country Life* magazine and television antique shows, the response to Southwell Minster is the same: Here, in a small Nottinghamshire town, is a hidden masterpiece, a secret waiting to be discovered.

It may seem strange to the visitor that a small town has such a large church. The size of the church reflects the influence of successive archbishops of York who were responsible for acquiring local estates from which the church and clergy derived their incomes and which enabled the Minster to develop to the size you see today.

The Minster was founded when King Eadwig (also spelled Edwy) of Wessex granted Southwell to Oskytel, Archbishop of York, by a charter of circa 956. A large Roman villa once occupied much of the present-day Minster curtilage. The location was ideal: Southwell lies in a shallow basin, enclosed by hills to the west and north and open eastwards to the Trent Valley. Water was plentiful, with many springs. A large part of the villa was covered when the Minster School complex was built over it in the early 1960s. In 2008/9 these buildings were pulled down and fresh archaeological investigations continue.

'Minster' means large or main church and, though Southwell Minster has only been a cathedral (the seat of a bishop) since 1884, the building dates back some 900 years. Construction of the present building, on the site of an earlier Anglo-Saxon church, was started by Thomas II who was archbishop of York from 1109 to 1114. The church is regarded as one of the finest examples in England of the Romanesque style of architecture, characterized by rounded arches. The iconic twin 'pepper-pot' towers at the west end are from circa 1160 to 1170, with the spires refashioned circa 1880. In medieval times archbishops of York regarded Southwell

Minster, along with Ripon and Beverley, as a 'pro-cathedral' with a seat for the archbishop. Southwell Minster served the southern part of the York province and, later, as a mother church for the newly-formed counties of Nottinghamshire and Derbyshire.

Unlike many of today's ancient cathedrals, Southwell Minster was never a monastery, which probably accounts for its survival through the turbulence of the Reformation in the 16th century. During the medieval period a collegiate church developed, with a Chapter of canons following a distinct set of rules. The canons gained their income from endowments of property and tithes, known as prebends, so the canons were also called prebendaries. By 1291 there were sixteen prebendaries and they made up the Chapter, the governing body of the Minster. Today, the prebendal system having been abolished, the Chapter is made up of the Minster's residentiary canons, along with representatives of the laity.

The Norman nave.
(Mike Kirton)

The font.
(Mike Kirton)

Blue-gowned Stewards are on hand to welcome you to the Minster, and it is well worth buying the small guidebook to enhance your visit. As you enter through the north door you will be struck immediately by the vast columns of the Norman nave, built circa 1108 - arguably the finest 'pocket' nave in the country. To your right, something completely different: the Great West 'Angel' window of 1996 by Patrick Reyntiens in muted tones that perfectly complement the soft honey-brown of the local Mansfield stone, from which the nave is built. Opposite you, the font from the 1660s with a Victorian wooden lid acquired to replace an original, presumably destroyed during the Civil War when, it is believed, the Minster was used as stabling for the horses of the Scottish Army.

Turn left and, as you walk towards the Quire, you see the glistening image on the east wall of the nave above the central arch, "Christus Rex", by local sculptor Peter Ball. Then you come to the central crossing - the transept - with, on your immediate left, the 2009 window

The medieval tympanum is a round-headed lintel above a doorway in the north transept.
(Mike Kirton)

commemorating the discovery of the original Bramley Apple tree in the town. The tree still survives in a private garden (see page 117). In the far left corner of the north transept is the tympanum, set above a doorway and certainly the most famous single item of carved stone in Southwell. Dated to between the 9th and 11th centuries and showing the Archangel Michael with a sword, a dragon and perhaps King David as a shepherd, it may originally have been part of a gravestone.

Opposite the tympanum doorway, down a few steps, is the Pilgrims' Chapel, built over what was once a baptistery using water from one of the wells of Southwell - a quiet space for private prayer and reflection. At the centre of the crossing, with one of the Minster's two main organs atop, is the Pulpitum circa 1335/40, built broad enough so that, originally, the gospel could be read from it and a choir sing from it. Through the gates in the centre of the Pulpitum is the 16th century northern-European brass lectern, dredged from the lake of Lord Byron's ancestral home, Newstead Abbey; presumably thrown there hastily during Henry VIII's dissolution of the monasteries.

Entrance to the Chapter House. (Mike Kirton)

Continuing eastwards along the left-hand side of the building, you come to the world-famous Chapter House of circa 1280. If your time is short, spend it here. The fluid carvings of plants, animals and green men are breathtakingly beautiful - and do look up to the star-shaped ceiling which, unusually, has no central support column. The Chapter House

An example of the Leaves-of-Southwell and one of the several green men in the Chapter House.
(Mike Kirton)

Carvings in the Chapter House.
(Mike Kirton)

One of many carved mice.
(Mike Kirton)

The Quire and High Altar.
(Mike Kirton)

The carved misericord (ledge), probably dating from the 14th century, of the Archdeacon's seat in the Quire. When the hinged seat is raised, the ledge allows support whilst the occupant of the seat is standing.
(Mike Kirton)

carvings have intrigued and delighted for centuries, with some claiming that the men hiding amongst foliage with their animals are a reference to the legend of Robin Hood, circa 1793! The celebrated artist J M W Turner RA sketched the exterior of the Chapter House and, today, the Minster has ambitious plans to improve the lighting, heating and interpretation of this remarkable space. For more information on the carvings see the *Leaves-of-Southwell* page of the Minster's website: http://www.southwellminster.org/leaves-of-southwell-2.html

Coming now to the east end of the building you reach the High Altar. Above it, on the lower level, are panels of some of the most important 16th century stained glass in the country, the work of the Parisian glass painter Jean Chastellian. Made in 1528 for the Temple church in Paris, they were removed during the French Revolution and ended up in a pawn shop, where they were purchased by Henry Gally Knight, a Nottinghamshire squire, who subsequently gave them to the Minster in 1818.

If you have young visitors with you, ask the duty Steward to tell them about the hidden carved-wood mice (by Robert Thompson) on the 1949 altar rails and furniture.

Crossing now to the right-hand (south) side of the building, past a fine Victorian monument to Dr Ridding, first bishop of Southwell, you come to the Candle Chapel, another quiet space where departed loved ones can be

The memorial window in the South Quire by Nicholas Mynheer. (By kind permission of Southwell Cathedral)

Fragments of Roman mosaic flooring in the south transept.
(Mike Kirton)

remembered. Going down the south side, you reach a fine panel of Roman plaster - mounted on the wall - from the bathhouse of the villa (see Chapter 2). The window to the left above the panel was installed in 2016 as a memorial to those fallen in or affected by the First World War. Designed by Nicholas Mynheer it is a Diocesan memorial, the boundaries of which, in the early 20th century, included Derbyshire along with Nottinghamshire. Back in the crossing, you come to the south door with, just beside it, the Bread Pews where a fragment of Roman mosaic can be seen under the floor. The bread pews were the place where, in the past, money and food were given to the poor and needy.

It may be that one of the Minster's choirs is rehearsing, or a service is in progress, during your visit. A choir of men and boys has sung here since the Minster's foundation. Today, there is also a teenage girls' choir and a chamber choir, the Minster Chorale. The Minster also runs a choral outreach programme to local schools. It has to be said that good behaviour by members of the choir has sometimes been

The Quire and organ.
(Mike Kirton)

found wanting. On an inspection visit on behalf of the archbishop in 1477 it was noted that the men of the choir should be "enjoined not to wear daggers in town, and to keep the peace". In 1478 it was no better, "*Cartwright and Lane suspended [from the choir] for striking one another - one with a dagger, the other with a club, in the churchyard.*" The choirboys, too, could be in trouble; in 1503 the terse comment was made that the "*choristers' vestments* [are] *disgracefully torn, they don't dress properly and want a good whipping*".

The Archbishop's Palace

Immediately opposite the south door of the Minster are the remains of the former Palace of the archbishops of York - the home used by successive archbishops when visiting the Minster and the area. An archbishop's residence at Southwell is recorded first in 1051 and then in the Domesday Book of 1086. Possibly, it was built using material from the Roman villa. Circa 1360 a new stone Palace was begun and, following various alterations, by 1452 took the form we would recognise today. In 1646 a large part of the Palace was badly damaged during the Civil War. In 2014 the ruins were conserved and the surviving built-section restored, with support from the Heritage Lottery Fund.

All the early medieval Kings of England from Richard I to Richard II stayed here apart from the ill-fated Edward II - doubtless as enforced and expensive guests of the archbishop of the day. In 1530 Cardinal Wolsey spent the final summer of his life at the Palace, trying in vain to appease the wrath of Henry VIII over the failure to persuade Pope Clement VII to grant the king a divorce from his first wife, Catherine of Aragon.

King James VI of Scotland admired the Minster and Palace as he travelled to London to be crowned James I of England, upon the death of Elizabeth I. His son, Charles I, used the Palace on many occasions and, after his capture in Southwell at the end of the Civil War, spent his initial moments of final captivity here. On the monarch's departure from the town as a prisoner, rioting caused the extensive damage you see in the ruined section today. The archbishops never used the Palace again.

*Remains of the Archbishop's Palace.
(Mike Kirton)*

*The surviving part of the Archbishop's Palace, which contains the
State Chamber on the first floor.
(Mike Kirton)*

If any one area of the Palace was to survive the rioting, it is lucky this was the first-floor State Chamber, arguably the most historically significant of all the Palace's rooms. Here, the archbishops deliberated and met with their advisers. It is believed the State Chamber was where the medieval kings slept on their visits and, in the 19th century, it was used as the 'Soke of Southwell' - a law court - as well as being part of a *'very respectable seminary for young ladies'*.

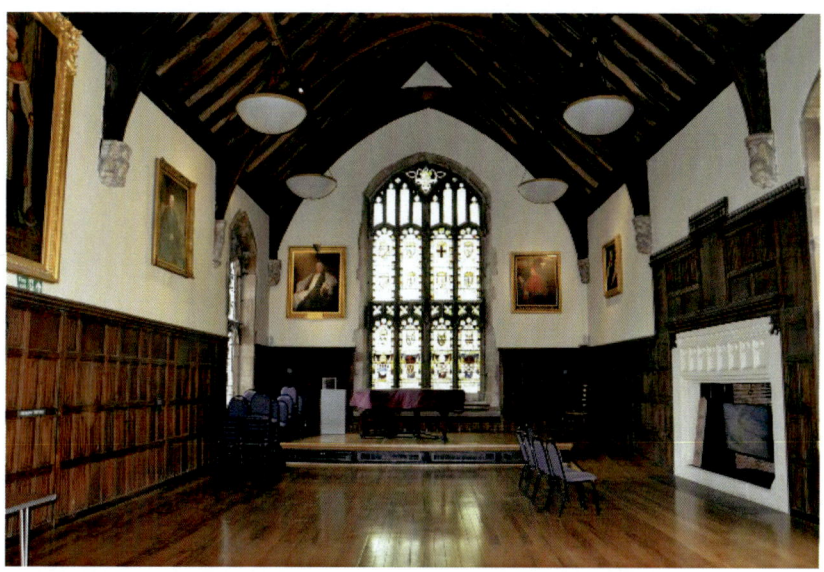

The State Chamber in the Archbishop's Palace.
(Mike Kirton)

Turning right as you leave the Palace, you come to the Education Garden. In 1108 Archbishop Gerard was found dead in his chair in the garden. When his body was moved, a book on astrology was found under his pillow - heretical studies in those days. His death was recorded, therefore, as being due to 'divine judgment for his addiction to the magical and forbidden arts'. In Gerard's day the gardens and hunting park were extensive. The present garden, created in 2014 from an overgrown coppice, includes individual planting areas reflecting the history of the Palace. The information panels tell you more. The development of the garden, with volunteer assistance, is an ongoing project. Between 1904 and 1907, a manor house was built in a corner of the Palace ruins, as the home of the bishops of Southwell, and this can be glimpsed from the Education Garden. Finally, turn right out of the garden and - to the east of the Minster - you find the satisfying symmetry of Vicars' Court, a group of five red-brick houses constructed in the mid-Georgian period to house the Minster's clergy and the Director of Music or *Rector Chori*, a function they continue to perform to this day.

The Minster's website is: www.southwellminster.org

The Residence at the head of the 18th century Vicars' Court,
Southwell Minster.
(Mike Kirton)

Chapter 4

The Minster School

David Hutchison

The present Minster School in Southwell is one of many large, co-educational comprehensives in England created in the late 20th century. Yet, it stands at the end of unusually long lines of development, which illustrate many of the landmarks in the history of English secondary education.

That history began with medieval grammar schools. The first Minster School may have been one of the earliest of these, perhaps initially teaching choristers from a Minster built soon after a gift of land, in 956, to the Archbishop of York by the Saxon King Edwy. There is documentary evidence of Minster clergy supervising grammar schools in Nottinghamshire in 1238 and proof that these included one in Southwell in 1313. That year *"Henry de Hykeling, master of Southwell Grammar School"*, was put in charge of the hospital of St. Mary Magdalen, Easthorpe.

Most early grammar schools operated within church buildings, and the earliest known location of the Southwell school was a chapel at the west end of the Minster. It also seems to have been typical of such schools in other respects. It had just one or two teachers and a small number of boys - though, for a few of them, it provided a route to university, with two scholarships created in 1530 to help ex-choristers attend St John's College,

The School's early location: in a chapel (now demolished) seen on the right of this 1775 print. (Private collection)

The Chantry Priests' House, situated on Church Street. The site is now partly occupied by Minster Chambers, formerly the Minster School. (Private collection)

Cambridge. Teachers usually charged fees, for which they were expected to teach religion and Classics. Minster records, in 1484, show clergy criticising the then schoolmaster, John Barre, as he *"gives time off ... to his scholars on whole school days, thus ... wasting their parents' assets ... and they do not speak Latin in school, but English"*. By 1579, those records also reveal school days were long: from late March to late September, *"six ... in the morning ... until eleven ... and ... one ... until six"*, five days a week, and *"every Saturday ... afternoon ... until evening prayer"*.

In the 16th and 17th centuries grammar schools often faced major problems due to the upheavals produced first by the Reformation and then the Civil Wars. In Southwell the former threatened its school's existence. Part of the income of some of its schoolmasters had been derived from also being priests employed to pray for the souls of the dead. In 1547 the government abolished chantry chapels where such prayers were conducted. It also disbanded the Chapter - the

The earliest surviving picture of a Minster School teacher or pupil: Magnus Jackson, Headmaster 1788-1809. (Courtesy Minster School)

group of clergy in charge of the Minster and its school - and it was only restored in 1557. The school, however, survived. A petition was drawn up by the churchwardens, seeking government help: *"We the poor inhabitants ... request that ... our Grammar School may ... stand ... wherein our poor youth may be instructed."* In 1548 the reply *"appointed that the said school ... shall continue and ... the schoolmaster ... shall yearly have for his wages £10"*.

The Civil Wars must have disrupted schooling in Southwell. Considerable damage was done to the Minster - probably by Scottish troops. The Chapter was again abolished (from 1649 to 1660) and the schoolmaster's salary fell into arrears. In 1652, however, Cromwell's *"Trustees for Plundered Ministers and Schoolmasters"* agreed: "[a] *yearly stipend ...* [shall] *be continued and paid to Mr Henry Moore, Schoolmaster ... together with ... Arrears."*

The 19th century was a much less troubled period for many grammar schools and they moved into purpose-built homes. As early as 1784 the Chapter decided that the part of the Minster, then used by the Southwell

The 19th century Minster School building (built 1819) - now Minster Chambers - occupying part of the site of the Chantry Priests' House. (David Hutchison)

school, should be demolished. Over the next few years the school occupied various buildings, including one that had once housed Minster chantry priests. In 1819, however, it was decided to demolish that and erect, on part of its site, a new building designed for the school. In recent years this has become Minster Chambers and the Minster Centre.

The acquisition of new buildings was often accompanied by a significant increase in the number of pupils. Yet, from the 1830s the Minster's school faced serious difficulties. The schoolmaster's "stipend" was no longer adequate, whilst government reform of the Church of England stopped masters supplementing their income as "vicars choral" (Minster priests) or absentee rectors. Competition from other local schools was also developing and in 1837 Minster choristers were moved to the small, recently opened Easthorpe Endowed School (now Easthorpe Hall). In 1858 the Grammar School closed down. It re-opened in 1864 but with only eleven boys, and its position was precarious until 1877 when it was agreed that John Wright should take charge. He brought with him his thirty pupils from the rival Southwell Academy on

A late 19th century photograph with headmaster John Wright at the back. (Private Collection)

School Photograph circa 1914, Revd J S Wright, headmaster, seated in the centre of the front row. (Private collection)

King Street. A description of the Grammar School in 1894, in the first edition of its magazine, "The Southwellian", at last reflected modest growth - to sixty-nine pupils (including once again the choristers) and seven staff.

Early in the 19th century the school had joined a trend to broaden the curriculum. English and Maths began to be taught and later, under John Wright, Agriculture, Design and Drawing, French, Geography, History, Music, Science, Shorthand, and Drill and Gymnastics were also on the timetable. In addition, team games (initially cricket and football) were introduced.

The next big changes the school experienced were due to the 1902 Education Act. This began the use of local taxation to support the provision of grammar school education. County Councils, as "Local Education Authorities" (LEAs), could now build new schools, but existing ones could also receive funding. In 1906 the Minster School became one of those. As a result, it was required to improve its accommodation - an extension to the school buildings being opened in 1908. In addition, in 1909 new regulations meant a few pupils, who were successful in an entrance exam, could earn a County Scholarship and a free place.

Soon after these reforms, war affected all grammar schools. Looking back in 1919, the Southwell Headmaster, Reginald Matthews, expressed particular regret that during World War One *"boys were induced by conditions of employment to leave school earlier than they would otherwise have done"*. In late 1945 he recalled that World War Two had led to some teachers leaving for military service (including *"Mr Eccles who died in action as a bomber pilot"*) and the arrival of evacuees - especially, in 1941, when *"we were suddenly asked to accept a hundred boys and staff of Worthing High School"*.

World War Two also created a widespread desire for a fairer society once peace came. One result was the 1944 Education Act which ordered free places in secondary schools be provided for all children for the first time. Initially there were fears in Southwell that implementation of the act might nonetheless mean the ending of LEA funding for the still rather small Minster School - after all, girls seeking a grammar school education already had to travel to Newark. Under Matthews's successor as headmaster, Basil Rushby Smith, however, it acquired "voluntary-aided" status under the act - securing continued LEA funding, even though the Church retained some control over its running. Meanwhile, pupil numbers grew (exceeding 200 in 1954) and in 1964 new school buildings were opened east of the Minster - with one peculiar feature, for a state-funded grammar school, a separate Junior Department which could teach choristers under the age of eleven.

Many of the new secondary school places demanded in 1944, however, would not be in grammar schools. They would be in "secondary moderns", catering for those who did not pass the "Eleven Plus" entrance exam for grammar schools. Secondary moderns replaced the higher years of "elementary" schools that had been providing education, for some older boys and girls, since the early 19th century. In Southwell the present Minster School has developed from the merger of the town's secondary modern and its grammar school. Thus its history includes the story of that secondary modern and two elementary schools.

Early elementary schools were created by church-run charities. They mainly catered for children below the age of eleven, but some of their pupils stayed at school beyond that. Until the early 20th century a few, aged thirteen to eighteen, even became "pupil-teachers", beginning to train for a career in teaching. Elementary education in Southwell began in 1840 in the Church of England's National School, on Nottingham Road (situated close to the Baptist Church and now a private house). The 1870 Education Act, however, ordered that significantly more school places be created to make an elementary education available to all. Often this led to the building of "Board Schools" - the first "state" schools in England. In Southwell, however, that was deliberately prevented because in 1871 a Wesleyan School was built on Kirklington Road - with Anglican assistance! (An image of the school appears in Chapter 6 p. 51.) According to the *Newark Advertiser*, "*The Church party met the Non-conformists in a very liberal spirit and offered substantial aid in their erection of a new school.*" At first both local elementary schools had pupil-teachers - the Wesleyan School, despite having only two adult teachers, was training up to three at a time. On the other hand, in the 19th century, both schools frequently recorded unauthorized absences by older pupils (often at work on nearby farms). Possibly the extreme

*The National School, Nottingham Road, circa 1920, now a private house.
(Picture the Past - see page 38)*

*Some National School pupils on their 'Annual Treat Day' circa 1910.
(Private Collection)*

case of that was one boy, aged 12, recorded in June 1891 as having only achieved 3 attendances in 23 weeks.

In 1957 Southwell acquired its secondary modern school, on Nottingham Road - the Edward Cludd School (named after a businessman who, some believed, had thwarted plans, during the rule of Oliver Cromwell, to demolish part of the Minster). It was co-educational, and later expansion was designed to enable it to cater for 750 pupils.

It was not an entirely typical secondary modern. Like the local grammar school it had links to the Church of England, being "voluntary controlled", and its first Chairman of Governors was the headmaster of the Grammar School. The brochure for its opening ceremony also seemed to suggest it was distinctively equipped to meet the needs of its catchment area, declaring *"the curriculum will have a definite bias towards life and work in the country-side"*, with pupils developing *"an ornamental garden and watercress bed as part of rural studies"* and *"an outdoor teaching space on the roof"*.

Part of the buildings of the Edward Cludd School, opened in 1957. (David Hutchison)

Like most secondary moderns, however, the Edward Cludd School had a short life. In 1965 the Labour Government instructed LEAs to plan for the introduction of comprehensives. Southwell's was created in 1976. The Grammar School marked its final year with performances in the Minster of Haydn's *Creation* and T S Eliot's *Murder in the Cathedral*. The Edward Cludd School organized a whole school day trip, by train from Fiskerton, to Skegness.

Edward Cludd pupils and staff about to board a train to Skegness, 1976. (Courtesy Newark Advertiser)

Stephen Pulford, last Grammar School Head, and prefects, 1976. (Private collection)

Whilst government influence over the type of schools in England had been growing during the 20th century, most English politicians prided themselves on avoiding the kind of state control, found for instance in France, over what schools taught. In 1988, however, a National Curriculum was introduced. In 1992 the Office for Standards in Education, Children's Services and Skills (OFSTED) and school league tables appeared. The Minster School, at first, seemed to cope with all this - regularly near the top of Nottinghamshire's league tables. Moreover, although a long tradition of providing some boarding places had come to an end in the 1990s, the number of its pupils was growing significantly. Yet, like many comprehensives resulting from an amalgamation of earlier schools, it suffered from inadequate buildings, and pupils and staff frequently had to travel between its two sites. Only after an OFSTED report in 2000, which judged the school to be "under-achieving", were new buildings provided. These opened in 2007, on a single site, immediately behind those inherited from the Edward Cludd.

Part of the buildings of the present Minster School, on Nottingham Road, completed in 2007.
(David Hutchison)

The new buildings helped the school become "outstanding" in 2011 and a National Teaching School (a centre for training new teachers) in 2013.

Despite obvious improvements in English secondary education during the centuries in which a Minster school has existed, there is a widely held belief that one thing was significantly better in the past than today - pupil behaviour. Some local evidence, however, casts doubt on that. For example, George Denison, who became a Grammar School boarder in 1814, later recalled the time when he *"threw a brass candlestick at the usher's* [assistant master's] *head" and thus "was taken to* [beaten] *... with an ash-plant"*. Indeed, as far back as 1503, Minster clergy complained that *"choristers ... rave and swear and disturb the priest celebrating our Lady's mass, and want a good whipping"*.

Acknowledgement

We are pleased to acknowledge the assistance of *Picture the Past* for allowing us to use the image of the National School.

'Picture the Past' is a not-for-profit project that aims to make historic images from the library and museum collections across the whole of Derbyshire and Nottinghamshire available via a completely free-to-use website. Containing more than 100,000 fully searchable photographs, postcards, engravings and paintings the website documents how life has changed in the region over the last few hundred years. You can visit the website for free at www.picturethepast.org.uk

Chapter 5

The Prebendal Houses

Susan Summers

A collegiate body, or chapter, was established in Southwell by the time of the Norman Conquest. This was the second phase in the Minster's development and an indication of high standing, subsequently acknowledged in the church's designation as the mother church for all Nottinghamshire. In common with administrative councils found elsewhere, including York, Salisbury, Lincoln and Wells, members of the Chapter were 'secular canons', ordained priests entrusted with duties in the conduct of services and the cure of souls. Living in the community they were distinct from 'canons regular', the likely incumbents when the church was founded in the 10th century who lived communally, adopting Saint Augustine's first rule in renouncing private wealth.

In addition to their Southwell duties the secular canons were also parish priests, supported financially by income from prebends - endowments of tithes, land and property. Known as 'prebendaries', they were independent landlords responsible for the management of their individual estates. How many were established during this early period is not known, but by the end of the 13th century sixteen prebends had been endowed. Named after their parochial estates, there were two exceptions: with no prebend of Southwell itself, most of its parish tithes were passed to the prebendary of Normanton; and Sacrista, not a prebend in the true sense since it comprised a house and garden in the minster town but had no parish tithes, land or property. Sacrista prebend's income, largely derived from church offerings, supported the Sacristan, a priest charged with care of the church, vestments, sacred vessels and relics, and much else. The dual role of other prebendaries meant that each initially maintained a parochial manor or parsonage as well as a mansion (also termed prebend) in Southwell in order to fulfil his responsibilities.

Sacrista Prebend.
(Mike Kirton)

    Situated some distance from main travel routes and removed from political strife, Southwell's church enjoyed security and was unaffected by organisational changes following the Norman invasion. Indeed, in 1171 a papal bull granted the Southwell Chapter spiritual and temporal independence, owing allegiance to none but the Pope. Although successive archbishops of York retained the privilege of appointing prebendaries, no defined position as head of the Chapter was established, the senior canon in residence carrying out the duties in rotation. This communal governance continued, unlike the hierarchy introduced in other major ecclesiastical institutions during the Middle Ages. In other ways, too, Southwell departed from accepted practice elsewhere: the most significant feature of its prebendal houses is the informal placement of the buildings, due to an absence of hierarchy and lack of firm control in the church's formative years. With no defined precinct around the Minster, these houses were detached within their own grounds and set back from the roads along the north and west sides of the churchyard, as clearly seen in the properties identifiable

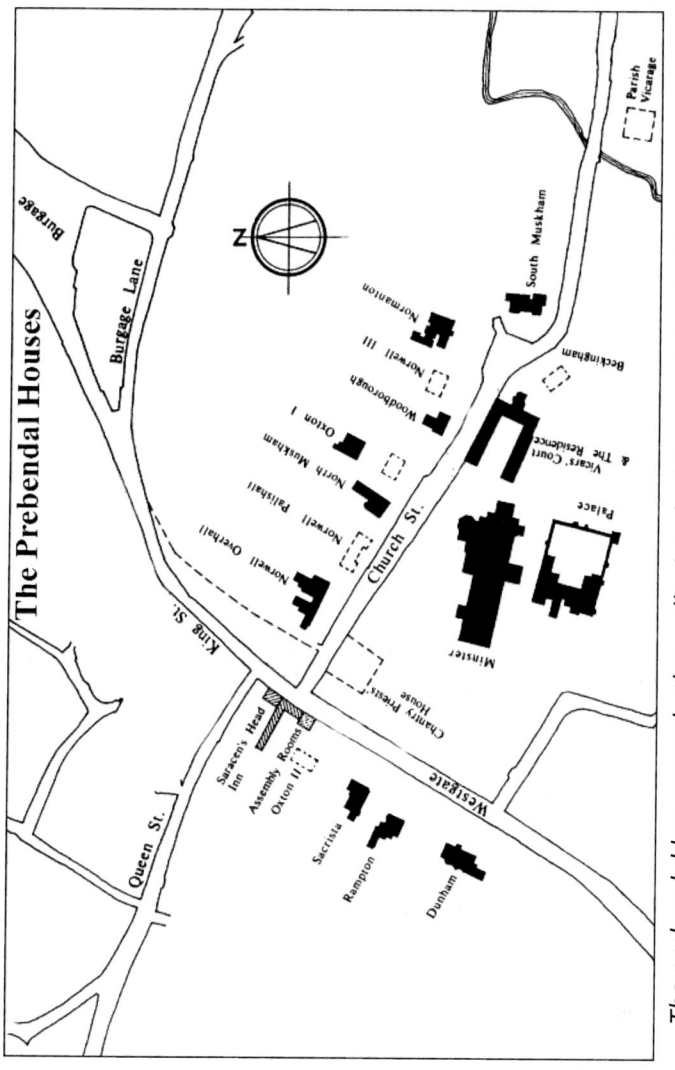

The Prebendal Houses

The prebendal houses and other collegiate buildings. Existing buildings are in solid; likely locations of buildings no longer standing, based on documentary evidence, are shown in dotted lines.

(Based on a map in A Prospect of Southwell, by N Summers, 1974)

today in Church Street and Westgate respectively. Had control of their estates not been in the hands of the individual prebendaries, their dwellings in Southwell may well have been enclosed in a cohesive group alongside other ecclesiastical buildings. By the time of administrative reform and later reorganisation of the collegiate establishment after the Restoration, it was too late to resite them in a more formal arrangement.

Of the sixteen prebendal houses recorded by the end of the 13th century at the height of their prominence, only nine locations have survived to the present day; three in Westgate and six in Church Street. Written evidence exists of two additional locations, Oxton and Cropwell (Oxton II) and Norwell Palishall. The earliest brick building in Southwell, Oxton II, was referred to commonly as the Red Prebend although its significance was later overlooked and it escaped listing as a building of architectural and historic interest. Consequently, there was no opposition to its demolition in 1970 to make way for extension to the Saracen's Head Hotel. The two houses either side of the car park entrance in Church Street together with a third, since demolished, and extensive outbuildings occupy land on which stood the original prebend of Norwell Palishall until the end of the 18th century. Records suggest likely locations for two other prebends: Norwell III further down Church Street where 'Edgehill' now stands; and Beckingham, across the road opposite South Muskham. However, the original whereabouts of the remaining three - Halloughton, Eaton and Leverton - are undocumented.

Another important feature is that the nine remaining prebendal houses are all replacements or remodellings of original buildings on the same sites, similar in retaining the outward appearance of country mansions of a modest scale but within a town setting, despite extensive internal alteration to some in recent years, and in the case of Norwell Overhall, division into two properties. On the north side of Church Street this former prebend comprised what is now the NatWest Bank and adjacent Minster Lodge. The bank's premises were largely rebuilt in 1960, but evidence remains of earlier high quality medieval construction in a section of rubble masonry and a 14th century window in Minster Lodge. Further along Church Street is North Muskham Prebend, which records suggest was rebuilt and restyled on several occasions during the late 17th and 18th centuries resulting in the present attractive frontage, although here no sign of the original medieval structure exists.

Lower down Church Street written evidence as well as design features imply that Normanton Prebend, with its impressive Georgian proportions and central porch of Roman Doric columns, was also rebuilt in the second half of the 18th century, whilst Woodborough Prebend with its well-proportioned and carefully detailed front elevation appears to be an early 19th century re-fronting of an older property (see over).

Normanton Prebend.
(Mike Kirton)

Until a fire in 2001, coupled with internal alterations to create several flats, indications of its late medieval origin, scale and layout of accommodation were clearly visible in South Muskham Prebend, despite the house having been extensively remodelled like so many others in at least two later periods. The outstanding original crown post roof structure also suggested the high quality of materials and workmanship in the earlier houses of the prebendaries.

Woodborough Prebend.
(Mike Kirton)

Prominent on account of its elegant Queen Anne design and proportions, it is likely that what is now Cranfield House was erected behind but within the overall site boundary of the earlier prebend of Oxton the First Part (Oxton I). Its fine classical façade is unequalled in the town. Ecclesiastical records of official visitations by the Archbishop of York in 1690 and 1693 refer to the ruinous state of Oxton I, resulting from both neglect and theft of its materials for use elsewhere. If this original conformed to the positioning of similar prebends in both Church Street and Westgate, it would have stood closer to the present road line. At the time of the new mansion's construction, most likely between 1700 and 1720, George Mompesson was prebendary of Oxton I. The architect's identity is unknown, but there are striking design similarities to Mompesson House in the Close at Salisbury, although the latter is on

Cranfield House, formerly Oxton 1 Prebend.
(Mike Kirton)

a grander scale with more elaborate detail. The change of name to Cranfield House occurred much later.

Of the three prebends in Westgate, Rampton, opposite the Minster entrance, has been remodelled several times, including later additions to outbuildings. At one stage drawings depicted the property with three steep gables and leaded sash windows reminiscent of the late 17th century. Next door the symmetrical regularity of 18th century classical building is clearly apparent in Sacrista Prebend's Gothic Revival exterior, although inside the corniced ceilings and curving staircase are simpler and late Georgian in style. An extensive rear wing was added subsequently. The oldest section of Dunham Prebend - now divided into apartments - is at the front, and dates from the late 16th or early 17th centuries. At this time the mansion was seven bays long, each capped by a single steeply pitched gable of that period. By the end of the 18th century the windows had been replaced with double-hung sashes and it is likely that this was when the gables were removed together with a row of attic windows, replaced by a roof parapet. Early in the 19th century a range of rooms was added at the rear with further alteration to the front, including the addition of the porch.

The underlying reasons for the remodelling and rebuilding of all these properties in more recent centuries are intrinsically linked to the history, administration and development of the Minster church in Southwell. The Reformation introduced a lengthy period of turbulence: at one point Henry VIII assumed the right to appoint prebendaries, whilst under Edward VI the Chapter was dissolved, its property passing to the Crown and the church reduced to parochial status. However, after 1585 a revised set of statutes granted to the Chapter under Elizabeth I paved the way for the establishment of a new college of sixteen prebendaries, although still without a dignitary at its head. In the next century the Commonwealth brought further disruption when episcopacy was abolished, only for the Restoration to herald extensive reorganisation of the collegiate structure which lasted until its dissolution in 1841. Subsequently the death of each canon resulted in the extinction of his prebend, the final incumbent dying in 1873.

The establishment of the collegiate body to administer the church in Southwell made it impossible for prebendaries to be in two places at once, fulfilling their dual responsibilities in both parish and minster. Duties elsewhere excused non-residence in Southwell, and leasing their mansions to lay tenants became a common practice, both an effect and a cause of increasing absence amongst the canons. Some went further, living at neither location following papal sanction in 1171, allowing the appointment of deputies or vicars at both the mother church and outlying parishes - vicars choral and vicars parochial respectively. Moreover, income derived from individual prebends differed; although direct comparisons are difficult, it is clear that even the best endowments at Southwell could not always on their own attract the most ambitious and able men. Nevertheless, the increasing practice of plurality of livings and acceptance of non-residence could offer substantial rewards leaving Southwell, although not able to compete in wealth and size with the great cathedrals, ranking highly amongst secondary ecclesiastical establishments in medieval England. Over an extensive period in Southwell's history the commitment shown by individual prebendaries towards their duties in the mother church was therefore variable: some incumbents such as William Mompesson of Normanton who supervised work on the new residence house at the end of the 17th century, and later still John Thomas Becher of South Muskham, were assiduous in carrying out their Chapter duties, the latter also renowned for his extensive public works. However, many who held appointments or more lucrative livings elsewhere contributed little, with

Rampton Prebend.
(Mike Kirton)

rare attendance at chapter meetings and the same names recurring regularly.

References to the poor condition, neglect and even collapse of various prebendal houses appear in records of visitations by successive archbishops of York. By the Restoration (1660-1685) many were leased to private individuals, but rentals were based on valuations of 1291, thus providing insufficient returns for adequate maintenance. The elegant prebend of Oxton I (Cranfield House) is the only example which can be positively identified as having been built by the prebendary for his own occupation after this date. However, lessees, increasingly gentlemen of some means, began to undertake at least partial restoration of their respective residences; from the late 18th century when tenure was more secure and long-term, many were willing to embark on more radical improvements. Finally, during George III's reign (1760-1820), the sale of church property was legalised, enabling the Chapter to clear the tax on the prebendal estates by selling the Southwell mansions, and the new owners to restyle, extend or rebuild them with confidence. Ever since, the majority of the former prebendal mansions have been in private ownership, the church's need for them having long given way to provision for a reduced number of vicars choral when they were allowed to marry after the Reformation, and accommodation for the senior canon in residence at the time.

Sources and further reading
Norman Summers, *A Prospect of Southwell,* Phillimore, 1974; Revised Edition, Kelham House Publications, 1988.
The Buildings of England - Nottinghamshire, Nikolaus Pevsner, 1951, revised by Elizabeth Williamson, Penguin Books Limited, 1979.

Chapter 6

The Methodist, Baptist and Holy Trinity Churches

Stanley Chapman

The Minster so dominated Southwell for many centuries that it must come as a surprise to many people that any Christian denomination other than the Church of England could obtain a foothold in the small and insular town. In fact, a range of religious movements from Quakers in the 17th century to the Salvation Army in the 19th century and Pentecostals in our own time have had a lively presence here. The vulnerability of the Minster was its ultra-conservatism, its somnolence for several generations, and the self-aggrandisement of the clergy hierarchy, so it was inevitable they would be challenged by fresher and livelier minds, especially in the period of religious revivalism.

Most of these Christian groups have not survived here, but three are still with us and have enthusiastic memberships in our community. All three have historic buildings in the town that will be of interest to visitors as well as local people fascinated by the story of our town. They are the Wesleyan (now Methodist) Church in Prebend Passage (to the rear of the Saracen's Head Hotel), the Baptist Church on Nottingham Road and Holy Trinity Church on Westgate. In this chapter, the story of each church is told in turn, focusing particularly on their origins and early connections.

The Methodist Church

By the end of the 18th century, the Evangelical Revival started by John Wesley had invaded most parts of England. Wesley visited Newark on several occasions, on one visit in 1787 (only four years before his death) he dedicated a new Chapel in Guildhall Street. Surprisingly, it was not from that direction that Methodism belatedly came to Southwell.

Non-conformity met serious opposition from the Established Church in our locality, exemplified by people such as William Neepe, an Epperstone gentleman farmer with family connections with Southwell (an ancestor had been a vicar-choral at the Minster, and master of the Minster School). He despised the open-air preachers to the extent that he once set a bull loose into a gathering of people who had come together to listen to the message. However, Neepe, aged thirty, had met his match. In 1800, attending a meeting with the intention of

William Neepe's house in Westgate, Southwell.
(Stanley Chapman)

interfering with the preaching, he found himself arrested by what he heard from Mary Barritt, a celebrated Evangelical preacher. The text was: '*Suffer me that I may speak; and after I have spoke, mock on*'. He discovered that Methodism was not what he had supposed: staying to a 'Class Meeting', he went home a changed man.

William Neepe heard a call to preach and conducted his first service in Farnsfield, but it was in Southwell that his greatest contribution was

*Southwell Methodist Church.
(Stanley Chapman)*

felt. The Methodist following there, unable to establish a chapel, had been meeting in a barn, with a half-barrel as a pulpit. It was only when a local tradesman found himself financially stretched, and needing to dispose of a plot of land with buildings in Westgate, he offered the property to Neepe, that progress became possible. In 1810, William Neepe set up both a business (a tannery) and a Methodist Chapel, together with a fine house, which still remains. The house (No. 81 Westgate) has its back to Westgate and is best seen from the path to Trinity Church.

Neepe's building, now demolished, served the Methodist community for thirty years. In 1811 a Sunday School was started, and it is recorded that in 1838 the 'Sunday School Procession' numbered 151 children and 16 teachers. The premises were quite inadequate for such numbers, and Neepe set about the work of finding a new site to build again. After setbacks, including the continued opposition of the Anglican Church, a plot was secured and the present building was erected, opening in 1839, the centenary of Wesley's conversion experience. Its confined location has resulted in some oddities of construction. The site was where the former stables of a house known as the 'Red Prebend' stood. The owner of the house stipulated that he must have an access drive, and the cottages alongside had to have their cart way preserved. House and cottages are long gone, but the cobbled cart way can still be seen, passing under the 'vestibule' of the church, which therefore meant that the Church gallery had to be built over it. The roadway had to be tall and wide enough for a laden cart to pass through. With no inch of space to spare, the builders went upwards. The three-storey construction includes a lower ground floor which is partially underground, and which was long used as the 'schoolroom' - the Sunday School of the Church.

The Wesleyan religious revival was mostly about attracting working class people neglected by the Church of England to the Christian banner. This is manifest in Nottingham and the industrial villages surrounding it. However, in Southwell and the surrounding rural villages the situation was quite different, as membership information shows. Of the original nineteen trustees of Southwell Wesleyan Chapel in 1839, eleven were farmers, mostly from surrounding villages where Methodism was already established. It seems that Neepe assumed the leadership of a mission that was already gathering momentum. Three other trustees were in transport, ideal occupations for transmitters of the Word of God. In addition, three local retailers and two craftsmen pointed the direction of the future growth of the church.

In their new home the Methodists thrived. When William Neepe died, his daughter Sarah became a leading force in the church community until her death in 1905. The 1851 census of religious worship records that at Southwell there were *'214 rented pews; the average morning congregation was 80 and the evening 250'*. In 1855 the 'Schoolroom' was let to a Mr Vasey for a Day School, and in 1870 the

Methodists themselves set up a day school in Kirklington Road. The building was used as a school until 1985 and still survives, but now as a family home.

The former Wesleyan Day School (1870-1985), Kirklington Road, Southwell. (David Huchison)

The Baptist Church

There are remarkable similarities and parallels between the history of the Wesleyan Church in Southwell and that of the Baptist place of worship. Both were overspills of religious fervour from Nottingham chapels in 1810; Halifax Place in the case of the Wesleyans and George Street in the Baptist case. Neither had a chapel building of their own in Southwell for several years, but the members were undeterred, meeting in barns on the Westhorpe fringes of the town for worship, and to hang eagerly on the words of passionate itinerant preachers dispatched to the new frontiers of the faith. Thirdly, both secured their own properties in 1839 after a long and arduous search, often menaced by the hostility of the Established Church. The surprise to modern ways of thinking is that the two revivalist movements did not make common cause in the town, but securing converts was the only thing that mattered in the heyday of the Evangelical Revival.

There were of course differences between the two churches. In particular, the Baptists were especially fortunate in securing the old Southwell parish workhouse, which had been built only 30 years earlier (1808) and included the attached governor's house, which was eminently suitable for a resident pastor. A photograph of the Baptist Church is on page 78.

At this period, The Revd John Thomas Becher, vicar general of the Minster, dominated both the civil and religious life of Southwell, and he did not hesitate to use all his considerable power to resist nonconformist encroachments in the town. As a magistrate and poor law reformer he was much the strongest force in the administration of the new Southwell Union workhouse, so it is a wonder that he did not intervene to stop the sale of the old premises to what he would see as an heretical movement. The Baptists must have felt confirmed in their faith that fervent prayer had induced God to be on their side, for he alone was capable of arresting Becher's perverse strategy. The Free Church movement in the unlikely centre at Southwell rested, as it must have seemed, on two miracles: the Pauline conversion of William Neepe to the Wesleyans and the submission of the mighty Becher to the Baptist assault.

The small Baptist cause in Southwell was driven on by the enthusiasm and evangelical passion of George Street Baptist Chapel in Nottingham. This hugely popular worship centre was built in the Lace Market, the focus of Nottingham's celebrity in the Industrial Revolution period, and its earnest membership included many entrepreneurs of this new industry and trade, who characteristically displayed as much energy in their religion as they did in business. In 1856 Stoney Street had 635 members who, in a couple of generations, had established 16 other Chapels in the surrounding villages and small towns with a total of 1,400 members, a sensational achievement. Itinerant preachers from the county town sustained numerous new causes, directed by preaching plans copied from the Methodist system. Stoney Street displayed its work by open-air baptism of converts, public spectacles that attracted crowds of onlookers, and were rivalled only by the witness parades organised by the Wesleyans. In Southwell's case, Baptist immersions were held in the Dumbles, a tiny rivulet that flows past Westhorpe and Westgate on a course now through Trinity Church graveyard. In this way, the age of evangelism was warmly embraced in Southwell despite the most powerful opposition - or indeed perhaps because of the implacable hostility of the Establishment in the town.

Holy Trinity Church

In the Church of England there are broadly two forms of public worship, the traditional sung 'high church' Eucharist where priests and choirs conduct the worship, and the more recent 'low church' so-called 'family worship' where the congregation joins the clergy in spoken prayers and in hymns. Not surprisingly, traditional high church worship is frequently found in cathedrals and other ancient centres of faith, and in the 19th century they usually resisted attempts to change to more popular ways of worshipping God. Southwell Minster was one of the bastions of the old ways, maintaining a system entrenched by lay canons who were paid to sing the liturgy, and a school to train boy choristers, who enjoyed a free classical education when that of all other children had to be paid for. Understanding these distinctions and partisanship is essential to the history that follows.

The Anglican challenge to the Minster came from a most unexpected source. Southwell appeared to be an enthusiastic exponent of the early Industrial Revolution, with two Arkwright-type cotton mills, a strong weaving and framework knitting colony, several malt houses, and a plan to canalise the River Greet to link the town with the Trent, then the M1 of the regional economy. However, much of this brave enterprise was soon aborted and by the beginning of the 19th century the little town was slipping back into its earlier position of rural backwater.

Despite the industrial decline, the enterprise of genteel inhabitants, the inspiration of a revived Minster School, and the location on good coaching routes were turning the town into a minor centre for upper middle-class education aspiring to the tradition of Winchester, Rugby, Uppingham and other school towns. Mrs Williams and her family determined to exploit this opportunity by establishing a boarding school for young ladies at Elmfield House on the Burgage. It became a successful enterprise under the leadership of her eldest daughter, Catherine Heathcote.

There is no record of why Catherine chose the evangelical course, but circumstances of the times indicate some probabilities. John Wade's *Extraordinary Black Book, An exposition of Abuses in Church and State* (1832) censured Southwell for its patronage and pluralism. The exposures of Archdeacon Wilkins in 1836 revealed that the Minster had sunk to such a low ebb that attendance averaged *only one person a day*. The neglect of the building in the long period of Becher and Barrow dominance, and failure of all reform attempts, is on record. The only solution for many church loyalists was a new church, a new endeavour that would be worthy of the sacrifices of missionaries spreading the gospel in the Empire. Catherine maintained a continuous correspondence with her brothers who were missionaries in New Zealand, and adopted the missionary spirit herself.

The momentum for a new church began with a leaflet circulated to all Southwell inhabitants on 3 April 1839 which maintained that *'the Choral Service is not suited to the taste, nor to the understanding of the majority of the people, who are not qualified to appreciate its merits, and that even those who prefer it might be benefited by sometimes hearing the service read'*, and proposed *'a Chapel in some central situation towards Westhorpe'*, a separate village from Southwell. This sounds pretty innocuous but it found no sympathy among the town's dominant families, or the Minster Chapter. In particular John Charles Wylde, Southwell's banker, would have nothing to do with the project, while Archdeacon Wilkins of Nottingham opposed evangelical ministry by proposing a new church in the High Church tradition as a chapel of the Minster. But 1839 had brought new challenges with the opening of Wesleyan and Baptist Chapels in the town.

After a sequence of setbacks, the persistence and dedication of the small evangelical band won the day. A new church in Westhorpe called Holy Trinity was built in 1844-6 for £2,500 of which Mrs Heathcote raised £2,000 with, the remainder (£500) being given by Henry Stenton, a local solicitor. The total figure included the land and £1,000 for the endowment of the living; the rest of the minister's stipend had to be paid for by pew rents. Heathcote's contribution is incredible when we calculate that her *gross* income from the school could never have been more than £800 p.a. (20 x £40 fees) and from that she had to pay teachers and servants. She certainly persuaded her friends to contribute (two families at Kirklington are mentioned in her letters), but most must have been saved from her modest income. We should let Catherine Heathcote have the last word. *'The building of this church has seemed to me to be a wonderful interposition of God for we have the powers of man to contend against as far as Southwell is concerned from the beginning to the end'* she wrote to her sister-in-law in New Zealand. In 1839, the centenary of Wesley's conversion, God finally smiled on the evangelical cause in Southwell.

Trinity Church, Southwell.

THE CEREMONY

OF

LAYING THE FIRST STONE

OF THIS CHURCH BY THE

REV. CHARLES W. EYRE,

RECTOR OF CARLTON, WILL (D. V.) TAKE PLACE

ON FRIDAY, THE ELEVENTH OF OCTOBER, 1844,

AT TWO O'CLOCK IN THE AFTERNOON.

(Stanley Chapman)

Holy Trinity Church from the rear churchyard.
(Mike Kirton)

The three churches' websites are:

    www.southwellmethodist.org.uk

    www.southwellbaptistchurch.co.uk

    www.holytrinitysouthwell.co.uk

Chapter 7

The Burgage

Ellis Morgan

If you walk up King Street from the centre of Southwell and continue over a gentle summit, you will find the view opens out into a pleasant green space of grass and trees sloping down to the crossroads below. This is the Burgage Green, a place popular with the townsfolk for strolling, walking the dog and playing informal games. From this viewpoint one can see imposing Georgian mansions, municipal Victorian buildings and small cottages surrounding the green.

The view down the Burgage Green towards Lower Kirklington Road. (Ellis Morgan)

In the past, however, this peaceful picture was often interrupted by livelier activities such as livestock sales, pony races and celebrations of royal events and great victories as reported in the Nottingham Journal of 25th June 1814:

Defeat of Bonaparte. 'Over 1000 persons gathered on the Burgage Green to celebrate this glorious event with a feast of Roast Beef, Plum Pudding and Good Ale. Later an effigy of Bonaparte, mounted on an ass, was conducted round the Green which after enduring the execrations of the crowd was thrown onto a large bonfire - a suitable reward for tyranny.'

A funfair visits The Burgage every April and September. The photograph dates from the early 20th century. (Southwell Civic Society)

The Ancient Manor of Burgage or Burridge

The green sits at the centre of the ancient Manor of Burgage (or Burridge) which lay north of the town centre between the River Greet, the Potwell Dyke and the Ropewalk. The manor was owned by the archbishops of York up to the 19th century and was administered by their stewards separately from the rest of Southwell. Records of the meetings of the Burgage Manor Court show that the green was used as grazing for livestock, and indeed this tradition continued until as late as the 1960s when Mr Cecil Hall grazed a small herd of dairy cows on the green.

Recent research into the Burgage area by Southwell Community Archaeology Group suggests that in medieval times, before the Georgian rebuilding of Southwell, the green may have been surrounded by cottage plots on both sides - we await confirmation of this when the results of three years of archaeological investigation into the Burgage are published by the group in 2017.

At the top of the green lay a medieval chapel dedicated to Saint Thomas the Martyr (Becket), which was demolished in the 16th century at the time of the Reformation. At the bottom of the green stood a hall or manor house (see Toad Hall below).

This pattern of a central green surrounded by cottage plots, a hall and chapel is very reminiscent of the planned manorial settlements of Yorkshire, many of which had their origins in the 12th to 14th centuries at a time when the Manor of Burgage was controlled by successive archbishops of York; a northern approach to settlement layout may have influenced this part of Southwell.

Gentrification

Starting in the 18th century Southwell underwent a major transformation with the building of Georgian brick houses, many on a grand scale. This gentrification was especially apparent on the Burgage where five large mansions set in extensive grounds were built, sweeping away many old cottage plots. These new mansions were home to a select coterie of wealthy families who came to dominate Southwell politics, both religious and secular. The extensive Becher family, related to Bristol merchants who had become rich through the slave trade, was especially influential, and none more than the Revd John Thomas Becher.

The last of these mansions to be built was Burgage Manor, which has the distinction of having been home to the youthful Lord Byron, the poet, and is a place of pilgrimage for Byron devotees and scholars.

Built for £500 in 1801/2, the original part of this handsome house was designed by local architect Richard Ingleman for Evelyn Falkner, the son of a wealthy local surgeon and apothecary. Falkner may have intended using the house as a boys' boarding school, but financial constraints appear to have obliged him to raise a mortgage on the house and let it for rent soon after its completion.

*Burgage Manor, home of Lord Byron 1803 - 1809.
(By kind permission of Geoffrey Bond OBE, DL.)*

From 1803 to 1809 Burgage Manor was home to Catherine Gordon Byron and her son George, Lord Byron, who was 15 years old when his mother moved into the house. The young Byron was shy and overweight with a deformed right leg and eyes of different sizes, not the picture one associates with the handsome romantic celebrity of later years. At the time Byron was a scholar at Harrow and later at Trinity College Cambridge and spent time in Southwell during the vacations.

Byron formed a close friendship with Elizabeth Pigot and her brother John, who lived in the large house across the road, now called 'The Burgage'. John was his companion on swimming expeditions to the River Greet. Elizabeth was several years older than Byron and appears to have adopted the role of an older sister, a role which continued for several years. She encouraged the young man to publish his first collection of poems entitled *Fugitive Pieces* in 1806 (printed in Newark). However, Southwell society, in the form of the Revd J T Becher (magistrate, senior clergyman and energetic reformer), judged some lines too erotic. On receiving this criticism, the young poet withdrew the publication; some of these early poems, however, appeared in a second collection of poems published in Newark the following year.

One of these early poems was entitled *To Julia*. Julia was Julia Leacroft who lived just around the corner at the top of King Street in the large brick house, now called Burgage House. Here Byron occupied himself with several amateur productions of theatrical pieces, which starred Byron, Julia and other local beauties. Such amusements provided the young man with ample opportunities to indulge his romantic nature. However, his interest in Julia provoked a sharp exchange of views with her brother, Captain John Leacroft, who was anxious to protect his sister's reputation. Apparently, Byron suspected a marriage trap and broke off further contact with the young lady.

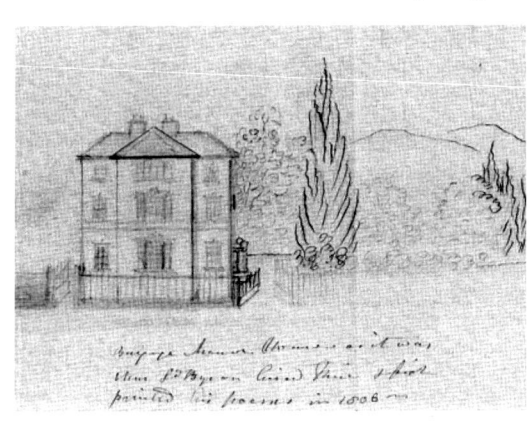

Sketch by Elizabeth Pigot c. 1806 of Burgage Manor.
(By kind permission of Geoffrey Bond)

A sketch of Burgage Manor drawn by Elizabeth Pigot in 1806 includes the location of Byron's bedroom on the first floor on the right side of the house; his view looking directly across the green would have been very similar to that of today with large brick mansions and small cottages. However, if he had looked down the green, he would have seen a very different picture. In Byron's time an old prison sat just beyond the Manor House garden. This was Southwell's first House of Correction, built in 1611. In Byron's time it was in a ruinous state; an official inspection in 1806 reported that *'nothing can exceed the squalid wretchedness and filth which are everywhere presented'*.

The young poet must have seen and smelt this decaying prison. Indeed, he may have had experience of the plight of its inmates in 1806 when his personal valet, Frances Boyce, was committed to the House of Correction for stealing four pairs of silk stockings; Boyce was later transported for seven years.

In a letter dated Feb 6th 1807 from Southwell to his friend the Earl of Clare, Byron writes:

"My time has lately been much occupied with very different pursuits. I have been transporting a servant, who cheated me, - rather a disagreeable event; - performing in private theatricals; - publishing a volume of poems (at the request of my friends, for their perusal); - making love, - and taking physic."

In 1809 Byron's mother left Burgage Manor and moved to the family seat at Newstead Abbey. No doubt Byron found Southwell and its society a rather restrictive stage, not helped by a somewhat tempestuous relationship with his mother, but he evidently formed some lifelong friendships here during his late teenage years. Byron's time in Southwell was at an important formative period in his life - a time when he took that major step of publishing his poetry.

In the 200 years since its first famous occupant the house has undergone many uses and a few alterations. Besides periods as a family home, it has at various times been a boarding school for girls and later for boys, a convalescent hospital for soldiers in the First World War, and a headquarters for an American oil company in the Second World War. On 22nd July 1944 Miss Sarah Lamport, representing the American Embassy, opened the Manor House as a Youth Hostel with room for 46 males and 34 female guests. In the Y.H.A. handbook for 1945 there is a stipulation that visitors should wear slippers - surely the poshest youth hostel in England.

In the 1960s the house passed back into private ownership. After several years as a Youth Hostel it was somewhat run down but has been lovingly restored by its present owners.

Further down the green

Further down the left side of the green from Burgage Manor is the Old Courthouse built in 1884. This now houses the offices of Southwell Town Council, but still has the old magistrates' courtroom upstairs and barred police cells in the basement. Continuing down the green is the Old Police Station, the Governor's House (a triumph of the bricklayer's art) and the old stone archway entrance to the 'new' House of Correction (see Chapter 8).

At the bottom of the green across Lower Kirklington Road are the old maltings. In the 18th and 19th centuries the brewing of beer was an important industry in Nottinghamshire and relied on a ready supply of malted barley, hops and good water. The Southwell area alone supported two breweries, eight maltsters, fourteen hop growers and osier holts for hop poles. The maltings on Lower Kirklington Road were built in the early 1800s; the main malthouse and workers' cottages are now private dwellings (see page 103). The old malt kiln survives and its roof is just visible behind the buildings. On the far right at the corner with Station Road is a detached house called The Brewer's House; this was the family home of Charles Walker who founded the maltings and was chief maltster.

Previously this site was occupied by an 'ancient timber mansion' called Toad Hall. The name is probably a corruption of 'The Old Hall', and this may have been the original manorial house for the Manor of Burgage. It was demolished in the 1790s to make way for the maltings.

Returning from the crossroads to the top of the Burgage green there is a war memorial cross dedicated in 1921 by the Bishop of Southwell; close by is a handsome brick mansion, Elmfield House. This was the earliest of the Burgage's grand houses, built circa 1730 for the Lowe family. From 1813 to 1905 it was a girls' boarding school, housing up to 30 pupils along with several servants and teaching staff. In addition to the usual range of subjects thought suitable for young ladies, such as French, music, drawing, painting and needlework, the pupils were also taught maths, science, history, geography, architecture and astronomy, a remarkably wide syllabus for girls at the time.

Elmfield House, as it is today and c.1920 before demolition of the outer wings. (Ellis Morgan and Stanley Chapman)

For fifty years the school was run by Catherine Heathcote. She had been widowed at a young age and devoted the rest of her life to the school and to fundraising for many charitable causes in the town - she alone donated £2000 towards the £2500 cost of building Holy Trinity Church (located on the west side of Southwell). Her death in 1881 was reported as *'the end of an era for the poor of the town who had lost a friend'*. She was buried in the grounds of Southwell Minster.

So the circuit of the green is complete. This is one of Southwell's secret places, most visitors to the town will focus on the Minster, the cafés and shops, but just a short step away is a peaceful green oasis - the Burgage Green.

Sources

Geoffrey Bond, 'Byron at Burgage Manor,1803-08'. *Transactions of the Thoroton Society*, Vol. 114 (2010), pp.147-157.
Stanley Chapman, 'Burgage Manor: New Perspectives on Georgian Southwell'. *Transactions of the Thoroton Society,* Vol.114 (2010), pp.135-145.
Megan Boyes, *Love without Wings. A Biography of Elizabeth Pigot* (Derby: Tatlen, 1988).
Betty M Arundel, *Southwell A History Walk* (Southwell: Civic Society, 2001).
Julie O'Neill, *The Life and Times of J T Becher of Southwell* (Nottingham: Self-published, 2002).
Southwell: The Town and Its People, Volume I (Southwell: Southwell and District Local History Society, 1995).

Chapter 8

The Nottinghamshire House of Correction: A Model Institution, 1611-1880

Robert Smith

Existing structures

The original Southwell prison of 1611 was completely demolished and replaced in 1808. Of the replacement, just the stone fronted reception lodge of 1808 and an adjoining brick governor's house of 1867 remain in their original forms on the Burgage. The outer shells of the three-storey chapel building with its arched windows and one prison wing have been converted to housing. Selected, previously demolished, wings are reflected in new housing structures and a circular roundabout epitomises the former superintendent's tower.

In all, at least nine original prison buildings no longer exist, but the international importance of the facility in terms of progressive penology still remains.

Origins

Imprisonment began to supplement corporal and capital punishments in the late medieval period and became more prevalent during the reign of Elizabeth I. As labour moved away from the fields in a process of urbanisation, town populations swelled and London became the fastest growing city in the world. This trend led to problems of vagrancy for those lured by false hopes of meaningful employment or trading. It is fitting that the first house of correction, created to clear the streets of idle humanity, was founded in London as Bridewell Hospital housed in a former palace of Henry VIII. Subsequent facilities were often known as Bridewells.

It was left to Elizabeth's successor, James I, to make it compulsory for every county in England and Wales to have a house of correction. Nottinghamshire responded immediately with an establishment at Southwell built in 1611.

The First House of Correction

The first Southwell House of Correction was built in 1611, but as early as 1656 the facility was in a ruinous state and much of it was rebuilt. After several visits by the famous prison reformer John Howard, and after an outbreak of fatal gaol fever, most likely epidemic typhus caused by the parasitic bacterium *Rikettsia prowazeki* transmitted by lice, fleas and ticks, further major improvements to ventilation, sanitation, separation of inmates and security were made in 1787. Howard had inspected just about every prison in Britain, most of which were

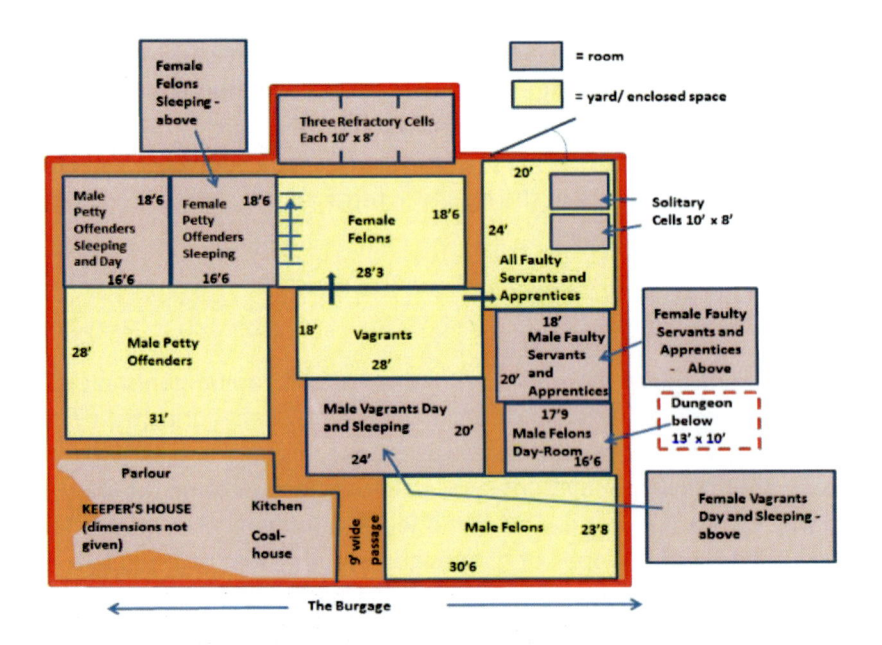

*1780s plan of the original House of Correction.
(Robert Smith)*

uninspiring and of a variable low standard. He found better institutions in Europe that he used as models to devise a uniform higher standard.

Local houses of correction in Britain had tended to be run as businesses where the keeper earned his living from the employment of inmates and fees charged for their upkeep and other services. Howard preferred keepers to be remunerated by a fixed salary to avoid exploitation and this change was applied at Southwell. Nevertheless, the then current and longest serving keeper, William Adams, continued to sell shoemakers' pegs at 3 pence per thousand from which he paid three halfpence to the prisoners. He used rooms intended for the proper separation of different classes of inmate for his own purposes, cramming all of the occupants into the dungeon and one or two small rooms while spending very little on building repairs and minimal sums on prisoner diets.

The New House of Correction

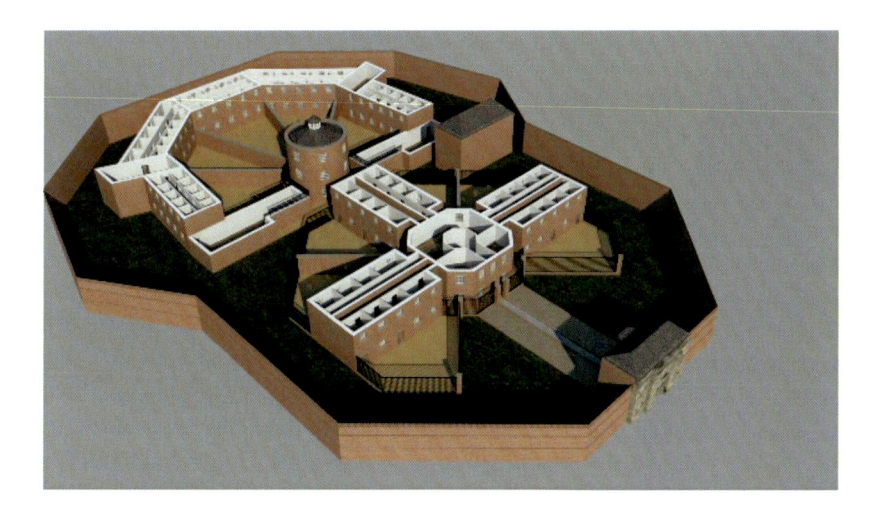

Digital reconstruction of the New House of Correction. (Created with the Digital Heritage Building Group at De Montfort University, Leicester and used to construct a 3D printed model)

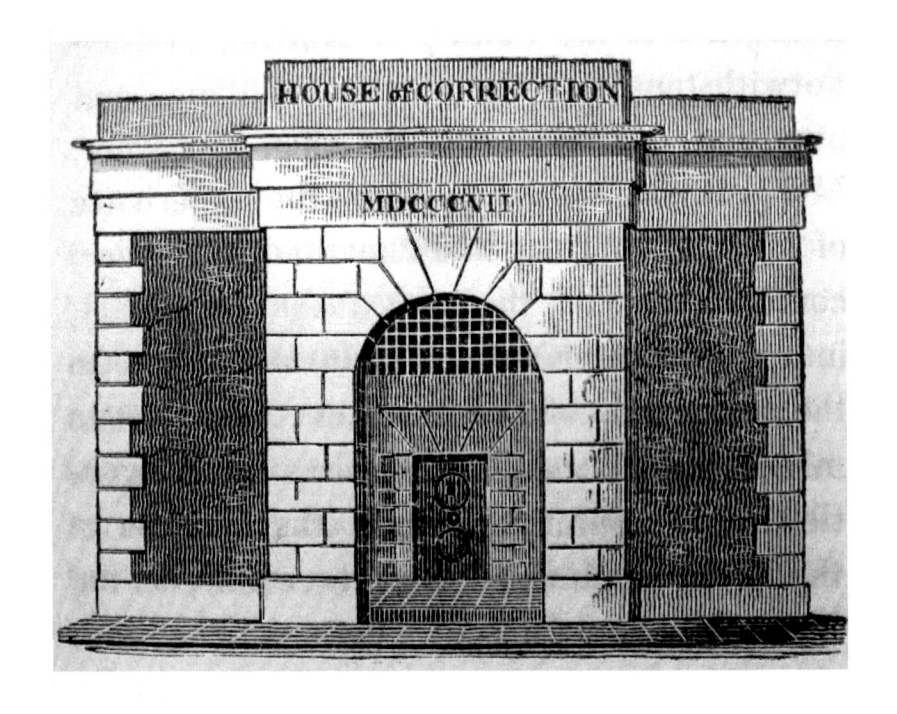

*House of Correction Gatehouse, architect's sketch.
(R P Shilton, The History of Southwell in the County of Nottingham, Its Hamlets and Vicinage ... S & J Ridge, 1818)*

By 1806 the old House of Correction was in such a lamentable state that, after publicly condemning the facility in his friend's column in the national *Gentleman's Magazine*, prison reformer James Neild persuaded the authorities to sanction a new larger prison to be planned by local architect Richard Ingleman. Local magistrate the Revd J T Becher concurred. Their lurid descriptions of the ghastly old facility are legendary.

As neighbours demanded too high a price for adjacent land, a nearby defunct brickworks was purchased. Neild recommended a radial (windmill) format based on Bury St Edmunds Gaol with three wings extending away from a central governor's house. Each wing was divided lengthways into two wards of six prisoners, with individual sleeping cells, a room doubling as a cell and infirmary, a communal day room, a general workshop and a cell for solitary confinement. The design was such that it enabled turnkeys (wardens) and the governor to patrol covertly and see into each ward and exercise yard and across to the boundary wall. Such lines of sight were all-important prior to the advent of CCTV.

Rules and regulations

If the architecture was state of the art, then the management regime was revolutionary. Based on the quiet reform of inmates, the rules were uniquely comprehensive, covering every aspect of prison life, but at the same time they were humane and respectful. Education and religious observance were important and there were rewards for compliance and hard work. Whilst there were punishments, there were rules for impartiality, sanctioning and proportionality. Fetters were rarely used.

National recognition

By 1811 so much evidence of reformative success had been gathered that Becher was invited to report to the first Parliamentary Committee on Penitentiaries. As a result the regime of communal quiet reform in place at Southwell was recommended nationally for the latter part of every prisoner's sentence, the first part being based on the harsher rules at Gloucester Penitentiary involving the individual separation of prisoners for most of the day and night.

By 1812 Becher had earned such a high reputation as a penal reformer that he was appointed a trustee and superintendent of the gigantic Millbank prison, the first national penitentiary situated on the north bank of the Thames.

Recognition in America

By the 1820s the United States was in such an unruly state that authorities looked to their prison service to restore order. They considered British practices to provide ideas for the way forward.

Extreme versions of the Gloucester and Southwell systems morphed to become the Separate System, based on total individual separation, and the Silent Congregate System, based on communal activity in complete silence. They were offered as alternative rather than complementary solutions, so an individual prison would be designated Separate or Silent Congregate.

Silence reintroduced at Southwell

In time, envoys from Britain and the Continent began to examine the extreme American versions and many recommended them for adoption by their respective national prison services. In 1835 Southwell acquired an extreme version of its own system, what they called the Silence System, based on practices at Wakefield Gaol brought in from the States. The measure had an immediate deterrent effect with intake numbers falling dramatically.

The 1818 extension

History tells us that Ingleman's radial format stood the test of time as it was recommended by the influential Society for Prison Discipline, remains in vogue today, and has since been copied many times. For his part, Ingleman was less than convinced when he prescribed the competing polygonal or semi-circular plan for a major extension in 1818. At about the same time he was constructing the large County Gaol at Salisbury, also on the semi-circular format, the extant drawings for which offer many clues as to the internal layout at Southwell.

Here the new five-wing extension, called the Penitentiary, housed an additional 50 prisoners of a more criminal nature, while the radial part was retained mainly for vagrants. Ingleman added his personal touches, including a walkway that facilitated covert warden patrols and offered better observation of the boundary walls.

A treadwheel in operation at Pentonville Prison from 1842, of a similar design to the ones in place at Southwell from 1823 to 1880. (Robert Smith)

Employment

From 1808, prisoners were usefully employed in the local industry of framework knitting which enabled them to earn money for themselves and something for the County towards the upkeep of the prison. Other light trades were carried on while some prisoners maintained the fabric of the prison and others were engaged in washing, cleaning, cooking and other tasks for the benefit of staff and inmates.

In time, the employment plan showed signs of failure as the prison began to compete for work against external businesses. As with many other houses of correction, Southwell was forced to implement non-productive hard labour regimes including treadwheels. In 1822, four wheels were installed, each 18ft 6in (5.5m) long and 5ft 4in (1.6m) diameter. They were housed in a two-storey building, two side-by-side on each floor. There were attachments should they ever wish to implement stone wheels for grinding corn, but the economics were never right for that. Later introductions were the crank, based on the turning of a handle, and the shot drill, where cannon balls were pointlessly carried from one place in the yard to another. All schemes were based on soul-destroying target numbers of repetitions over an entire working day.

The implementation of the treadwheels coincided with the arrival of a new governor, Matthew Mole, in December 1822. He had a military engineering background and was able to progress the difficult introduction of the treadwheels and engage in many practical duties at the prison. This included the addition of a third storey to all but one of the eight wings of the prison, including a new chapel on the third wing of the Penitentiary. Another project included the conversion of space between the 16ft (4.9m)-deep foundation walls of the treadwheel house for a bakery operated by prisoners.

Cell door found during excavations in 2015. (Mike Kirton)

Given their allegiance to reformative imprisonment, it is somewhat surprising that the Revd J T Becher, Governor Mole and Visiting Surgeon Benjamin Hutchinson were greatly in favour of the treadwheel. This was demonstrated when they engaged in a national debate after government medical advisors had decried what they claimed were the injurious effects of the machines. The Southwell management conducted trials with prisoners, the results purporting to show that the effects were, for the most part, beneficial. The trial findings were submitted to an inquiry and published nationally. Hutchinson committed their observations to print in, *Observations on Prison Discipline etc. (S & J Ridge, 1823).*

Dismissal of Matthew Mole

The three Southwell officials, Mole, Hutchinson and Becher, worked well together for several years and the surgeon was always a great supporter of the governor. Unfortunately, in time, a rift developed between Becher and Mole and the latter was constructively dismissed. He was accused by Becher of misappropriating certain monies belonging to prisoners and permitting his wife to gossip around the town about confidential prison matters. Outgoing Mole published a book entitled *Eleven Years' Governorship of Southwell House of Correction* (J Dunn, 1834) in which he described what he considered to be underhand treatment and made a claim for reinstatement. He never returned to the job, but his book and Hutchinson's *Observations on Prison Discipline* (S & J Ridge, 1823) have proved to be extremely valuable sources of detail regarding the operation of the prison during a formative era.

Cases and incidents

The prison was intended mainly for vagrants and petty criminals and as such rarely attracted those convicted for extreme crimes, except some awaiting trial. Henry Standley had been held at Southwell pending trial for a particularly brutal murder. The stories he told in defence became ever more fanciful and in the end he realised that he stood no chance of avoiding his ultimate demise. He decided to take his own life and such was the ill feeling against him that, in the presence of a large crowd, he was buried at the busy nearby crossroads where he would never rest in peace.

There was the thief who would not have stolen a shirt had he noticed that it was designed for a woman, and Isaac Holden who used a 29-verse poem to describe his multiplicity of crimes by way of confession. Byron's footman was sentenced to seven years' transportation for stealing four pairs of the poet's stockings. In 1839 H B died from consuming Monk's Hood (*Aconitum napellus*) taken from the governor's garden, and in 1849 F395, T L, a boy of 17, was crushed to death trying to retrieve an object from under a treadwheel.

Replacement wing, 1867

During the latter half of the 19th century, local prisons became subject to ever more stringent controls imposed by central government, including loss of grants for non-compliance. Measures included increased separation of individual prisoners in cells designed to conform to a certain standard. The radial part of the Southwell prison was no longer compliant, and in 1867 this section of the prison was demolished and replaced with a large multi-storey block partly built using prison labour.

Closure

Central authorities recognised that locally run prisons often experienced excessive capacity and began to insist on reciprocal arrangements with nearby facilities. Firstly, arrangements were made between prisons within Nottinghamshire, and then between Nottinghamshire and Lincolnshire. A numbers game ensued with the result that long-term excessive capacity was identified and certain prisons were earmarked for closure. Despite central recognition for Southwell as being the best prison in Nottinghamshire, it was finally ordered to close in February 1880. Subsequent uses of the site for lace making and freight services are covered elsewhere in this book (Chapter 11).

The remaining Gate House, which bears a memorial to the sixteen men of Carey & Co Ltd who lost their lives in the First World War. (Mike Kirton)

Chapter 9

The Workhouse

Victoria Preece

Under the Old Poor Law, passed in the reign of Elizabeth I, each parish was responsible for their own poor. The cost of caring for the poor was paid by a tax on those who owned property, 'the ratepayers'. Poorhouses were established in the parishes, and outdoor relief, help to the poor in their own homes, was also paid. This system survived for over 200 years, but by the start of 19th century it was beginning to break down as costs rose. The total cost for all poor relief in England and Wales rose from £4 million to nearly £8 million between 1803 and 1818. This was mainly the result of increased unemployment caused by land enclosures, mechanisation, and a rising population, which led to riots as workers felt threatened financially.

The Original Workhouse on Nottingham Road, now the Baptist Church. (Victoria Preece)

Origins

Many schemes to help the poor were tried throughout the country. Here in Southwell, in 1808, the Revd John Thomas Becher, vicar general at the Minster, opened a workhouse on the Nottingham Road, where he put into practice his ideas about caring for the poor. He believed in stopping outdoor relief and bringing all those who needed help into the workhouse. Children, the old and the infirm were to be treated kindly, but the able-bodied were to be treated harshly. The belief that poverty was the fault of the individual was prevalent at that period, viewed as idleness and indolence. Becher saw the Southwell Workhouse as a success. The local poor rates dropped by 75% in three years. In 1824 a second workhouse was built in the parish of Upton under Becher's leadership; costs were spread between the forty-nine parishes around Southwell. This second workhouse, the one we see today, was known as the Thurgarton Hundred Incorporated Workhouse, used the same system of admission and treatment as the Southwell Workhouse.

Southwell Workhouse.
(Victoria Preece)

In 1828 Becher wrote a pamphlet, *The Anti-pauper System: Investigation into the Effects of the Poor Laws*. He described his experiment with the small workhouse in Southwell and his encouragement of forty-nine surrounding parishes to copy his scheme in a larger workhouse. He stressed the reduction of the poor rates and *'improving the moral demeanour'* of the poor by giving them a purpose-built house. The new building, with its high walls, was to be seen as a deterrent. A Royal Commission set up to investigate the administration of the poor laws was impressed. Becher's system became the basis for the Poor Law Amendment Act of 1834. After the passing of the Act, the Southwell Workhouse joined the Thurgarton Hundred Workhouse becoming the Southwell Union Workhouse in 1836. The small Southwell workhouse was sold and converted into the Baptist Chapel. The new system required groups of parishes to join together into unions to build their workhouses. There would be one workhouse every 20 miles or so. By 1839 there were almost 600 workhouses in England and Wales.

Segregation and daily routine

Men, women and children were placed into different parts of the Workhouse. The supervision, classification and segregation regime was intended to act as a deterrent. Help for the poor would thus be restricted to the workhouse alone, doing away with outdoor relief. This was never achieved and about 80% of relief continued as outdoor relief.

On admission to the Workhouse each pauper was inspected by the Medical Officer who decided which class they should enter. The old and infirm did not have to work and were given extra rations and treats such as tea, cheese, butter, beer, and the old men had tobacco. Able-bodied paupers, on the other hand, would be made to do degrading, arduous and often useless work. The men broke stones that were sold to spread on the roads and did the gardening as the workhouse grew all its vegetables. They ground bones from the kitchen for fertiliser and emptied the privy pits, using the excrement as manure for the gardens. They painted the house inside; records show that lime wash paint was bought twice a year. The men also made the bread for the workhouse and the oven is still in one of the back rooms in the men's work yard.

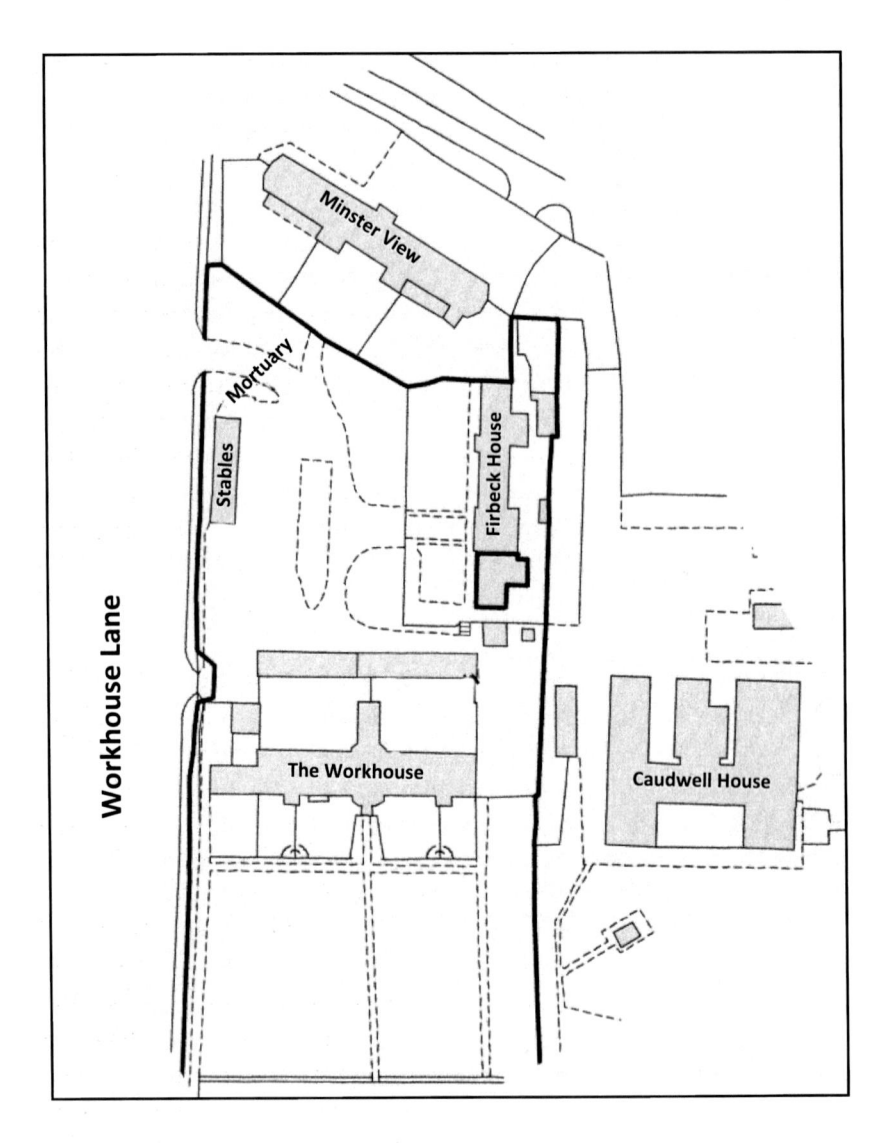

*Plan of the Workhouse.
(Courtesy of The National Trust)*

Money for old rope - oakum.
(Victoria Preece)

A dining table at the Workhouse.
(Victoria Preece)

Both men and women picked oakum, which was a hated job. Old naval rope would be picked clean of tar, salt and all other dirt, then unwound and teased out into fine threads of hemp, called oakum. This was sold back to the naval shipyards where it was stuffed between the planks of the wooden ships and covered with pitch, caulking the vessels. The old rope was bought by the workhouses for £3 a hundredweight (51 kg) and the oakum was sold for £5 a hundredweight, money for old rope! Work done by the women comprised household chores - cleaning, cooking, mending, darning, washing, and nursing the old and the sick. There was no paid nurse until 1869 when the Matron's daughter was appointed with no training.

The paupers' day started at 6 a.m. in summer and 7 a.m. in winter. They dressed, tidied the dormitory, and went to their day room for morning prayers. Breakfast consisted of gruel, bread, and water to drink. An able-bodied man would get 1 quart (1.1 litres) of gruel and 6 oz. (170 g) of bread. They then worked until 12 noon when they stopped for dinner, the main meal of the day. Meat and potatoes were served three days a week, and vegetable broth on three others. On Saturdays there was a suet pudding filled with all the leftovers from the week. On a meat day a male able-bodied pauper would get 5 oz. (142 g) meat, 1 lb (454 g) potatoes, and 6 oz. (170 g) bread. Work started again at 1 p.m. and continued until 6 p.m. when supper was served; the same as breakfast. On Sundays only necessary work was done and the paupers attended divine service in the Committee Room. There were two services, one for men and one for women. Children were walked to Upton Church for divine service.

Masters and Matrons

The workhouse had a small staff, with a Master and Matron to run the house who reported to the Board of Guardians, elected representatives from each of the parishes, plus JPs who lived in the union. Master and Matron were mostly married couples. Some stayed for a short time, 2 or 3 years. Others, such as the Weightmans, were there much longer, 13 years. Thomas and Mary Weightman came to the Southwell Workhouse in 1838. The Master and Matron's joint salary was £50 a year, with lodgings and food provided. Thomas was frequently in trouble for keeping his books incorrectly.   The Weightmans were asked to resign in 1839 for inadequately kept books, but no one applied for the post, so they were retained.

Children

There was no mention of children in the 1834 Poor Law Amendment Act. A survey in 1838 showed that half the population of the workhouses in England and Wales were children. Many workhouses, including Southwell, employed schoolteachers. After the survey an education programme became compulsory. It was ordered that education *'should be practical so as to fit them for their humble role in society'.* Children did not work, but had instruction in the schoolroom for about 3 hours a day, and were also taught skills such as cobbling and gardening for the boys and household skills and dressmaking for the girls. Babies stayed with their mothers from birth until 2 years old, then they joined the children in a mixed group to the age of 7 years. Thereafter they were segregated by gender, becoming adults at the age of 13 for boys and 15 for girls.

Schoolteachers

The provision of teachers was the 'Achilles Heel' of workhouse education. Recruitment, quality and retention of teachers were problematic. Teaching was not regarded as a prestigious occupation - rated lower than village tradesmen such as the blacksmith or butcher. Maria Richardson was appointed schoolteacher in 1842 at a salary of £15 a year, including food and accommodation. She was the first teacher to have a teaching certificate, but the Inspector of Schools reported she was not very good. In 1850 a schoolmaster, 21-year-old William Sumner, was appointed with a salary of £20 per annum. He worked with Miss Richardson who was then 38 years old. On 24th September 1851 Miss Richardson resigned *'having lost the use of her right hand'*. A month later, the Master's Journal informed the Guardians that she was *'in the family way, and she was old enough to be his mother!'*. Mr Sumner resigned 3 weeks later.

Women's Work Yard.
(By kind permission of the National Trust)

The Paupers

Unfortunately, the Southwell Workhouse admission and discharge documents have not survived. Some paupers are known from the Guardians' Minutes, the Master's Punishment books, letters to the Poor Law Board, and the local papers. Here are two examples:

Sara Godson, an able-bodied pauper was always in trouble. She was born in 1836 in Sutton-on-Trent. In the 1851 census she is recorded as being employed as a servant in Marnham. By 1854 she is in the workhouse and is regularly in the punishment book:

> *22nd May: Misbehaving during divine service. 2 hours in the refractory ward.*
> *29th August: Getting over the yard door with the intent of getting away. Stopped her porridge at supper.*
> *1855*
> *5th February: Assaulting one of the other inmates and singing songs nearly the whole day. No punishment reported.*
> *16th March: Getting over the fireguard and using abusive language to the matron. No punishment recorded.*
> *12th March: Misbehaving during Divine Service, afterwards fastening the door of the day room so that the other inmates could not get in. 3 hours in the refractory ward.*

Was Sara a trouble-maker or were there other problems? It was found later that she was admitted to the County Lunatic Asylum in 1857 and remained there until her death in 1859.

John Fogg was a labourer in Sutton-on-Trent. In 1847 John killed and stole a sheep. When the constable arrived at his cottage, his wife said he was in bed. The constable went to the bed where John was lying, pulled back the clothes to find the parts of the dead sheep lying between the mattress and the bed frame. He was found guilty of sheep stealing in the Nottingham County Assizes on 2nd July 1847 and was sentenced to transportation. Fogg was held first in Nottingham jail, then in Millbank, London, and subsequently on a hulk ship at Portsmouth. He sailed for Australia on 1st January 1850, arriving on 30th April when he started his sentence. His wife and children, having no support, were admitted into the Workhouse. His sentence was completed in 1854. By 1855 John had saved enough to pay towards the cost of the voyage and the family emigrated to Australia to join him. He died in Queensland in 1864.

The 20th Century

By 1913 workhouses were called Poor Law Institutions and Southwell Workhouse was renamed Greet House. An Infirmary had been built on a site adjacent to the Workhouse in 1871 and in 1914 the Infirmary, Firbeck House, was extended at a cost of £900 to provide living accommodation for the children. However, by 1924 further infirmary space was needed and Minster View was planned, built, and opened in 1928, costing £10,000 for the building and £1,500 for furnishings. Patients moved over to Minster View leaving more space for the

Bedroom for the homeless at the Workhouse, 1970s.
(Victoria Preece)

children. Caudwell House was built close by in 1937 as a children's home and all the children moved there from Greet House, but their mothers lived in Firbeck House.

In 1929 the functions of the Poor Law were transferred to local authorities and the Southwell Workhouse came under Southwell Rural District Council.

After World War II, Minster View was used as a hospital, and Firbeck House became a home for the elderly. The Poor Laws were repealed in 1948, when the Welfare System began.

In 1964 the few men in Firbeck House were moved to other institutions. Firbeck House became available for 'less confused old ladies' and Minster View for 'mentally infirm women'. During the 1960s and 1970s some rooms in the Workhouse were used to house homeless families - mothers and children only - and in 1974 the new Newark District Council took over the homeless accommodation. By 1995 a care home was opened in Newark and all the remaining elderly residents were moved there.

The National Trust bought the Workhouse in 1997 and opened it to the public in 2002.

Conclusion

The Workhouse system was never intended by its founders to be cruel; it aimed to be fair and efficient but is regarded with horror by the general public. It must be seen as the first national attempt at a programme of social welfare. Workhouses catered for more than the unemployed; they cared for the old, the sick, the mentally ill, and the orphans at a time when other help was rarely available. The New Poor Laws, the first of which was the 1834 Poor Law Amendment, paved the way for the Welfare State and the National Health System. Many modern hospitals, such as Nottingham City Hospital, were built on the sites of the old workhouses they replaced.

I would like to thank the Workhouse research group for the free access they gave me to their research, particularly Derek Wileman who read and corrected my work.

Chapter 10

Southwell's Inns and Alehouses

Roger Dobson

Why did Southwell have so many inns and alehouses?

From existing evidence, there have been at least thirty licensed inns, alehouses, beerhouses and breweries in Southwell over the years. This does not include the numerous wine and spirit merchants and malthouses that also existed in the town. Today, many fewer hostelries remain at a time when the population is nearly three times what it was in 1850. In medieval times ale was regarded, with good reason, as a healthier alternative to water. Water supplies were often contaminated and it was common for women and even children to drink weak ale. This meant that, apart from the local hostelries, many people who could afford the equipment brewed their own ale at home. It also seems likely that Southwell had a large number of inns and alehouses to service the pilgrims and visitors attracted to the town by the Minster, many of whom required food and lodgings in the town.

Inns and alehouses were visited when people from neighbouring villages flocked into the town to celebrate major events such as royal births, coronations, the king's birthday and key military and naval victories. Local people also frequently attended the town's fairs, markets and horse races. Inns were the traditional venues for meetings and annual dinners of local clubs and societies, ranging from groups of clergy, freemasons and the military to friendly societies, trade and floral clubs. In the absence of specialised facilities, such as a leisure centre or individual clubhouses, publicans were keen to promote sports on their premises. The Crown and the White Swan promoted cockfighting, providing the pit, pens for the birds and, of course, refreshments. The Crown was also the centre for prize-fighting and the White Swan promoted horse racing on the Burgage.

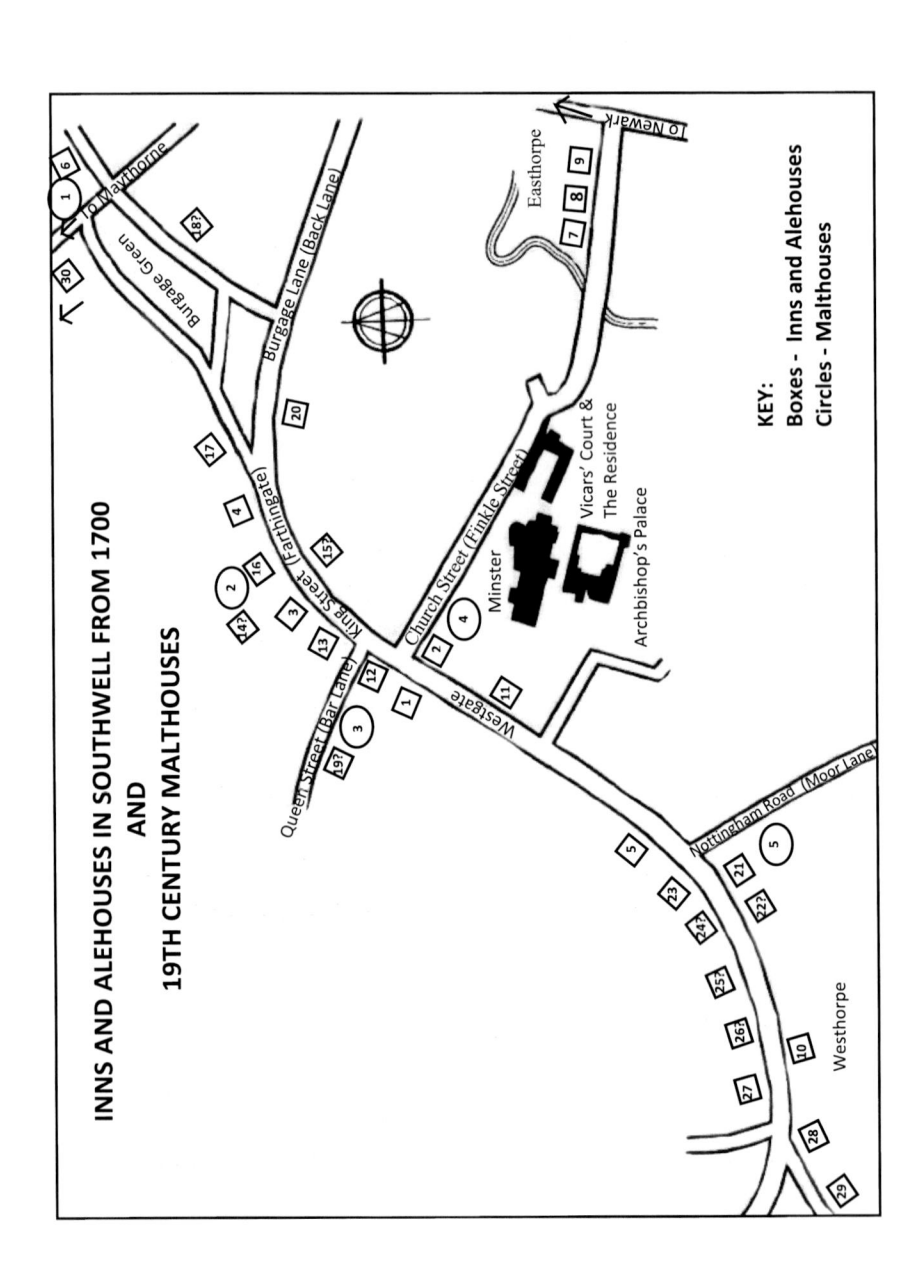

INNS AND ALEHOUSES IN SOUTHWELL FROM 1700 AND 19TH CENTURY MALTHOUSES

KEY:
Boxes - Inns and Alehouses
Circles - Malthouses

KEY TO INNS, ALEHOUSES, BEERHOUSES, INSTITUTE AND MALTHOUSES

Surviving Inns and Public Houses 2016:

1. Saracen's Head (King's Arms)
2. Crown Inn
3. Admiral Rodney Inn
4. Wheatsheaf
5. Reindeer Inn
6. Final Whistle (Newcastle Arms)
7. Bramley Apple (George & Dragon)
8. Hearty Goodfellow
9. Old Coach House (White Lion)

Lost Inns, Alehouses, Beerhouses and Breweries:

10. Dumbles (Admiral Nelson)
11. Castle Inn
12. Cross Keys Inn
13. Black Bull Inn
14. Southwell Brewery
15. King Street Beerhouse
16. Portland Arms
17. White Swan
18. Boot & Shoe Alehouse
19. Bar Lane Beer House
20. Black Horse Beerhouse
21. Westgate Brewery
22. Bear Alehouse
23. Shoulder of Mutton
24. Woolpack Inn
25. Westgate Beerhouse
26. Red Lion
27. Grapes Beerhouse
28. Westhorpe Beerhouse
29. Workman's Rest Institute
30. William IV B/house, Maythorne

Malthouses in the 19th century - likely locations:

1. Charles Walker
2. John Maltby
3. John Nall
4. W Smith (Crown)
5. Ealand's Westgate Brewery

SOUTHWELL COCKING.

NOTICE is hereby given, that there will be a Main of sixteen Cocks, fought at the Red Preband, Southwell, on the 15th Day of April, 1782, for a Mare, or Ten Pounds in Money value. Each Subscriber to put in Half a Guinea and the Winner to pay to the second best Twenty Shillings, and to the Third and Fourth Cock Ten Shillings each. No Cock to exceed the Weight of Four Pounds Six Ounces. The first Pair of Cocks to be on the Pit at Twelve o'Clock. To Fight in Silver.

*** A genteel Ordinary will be provided at the CROWN. STATHEM and GOODWIN, FEEDERS.

'Southwell Cocking' advertisement. (Nottingham Journal 6 April 1782)

In *White's Trade Directory* of 1822 nine new beerhouses are shown in Southwell, representing a dramatic increase in the number of licensed premises. Several of these beerhouses were located in workshops where craftsmen sold ale to waiting customers. By 1830 Parliament was concerned about the high level of gin drinking and its effects on the working classes, so it passed a law (the 1830 Beerhouse Act), which encouraged people to drink beer rather than gin. All duty on beer was abolished and any householder had the right to sell beer upon the purchase of a two-guinea licence from the Excise Office.

However, the Temperance Movement's strong opposition to the drink trade had begun to influence central government's attitude to the growth of public houses, and in 1869 beer houses, like all public houses, had to apply to the local magistrates for licences. Magistrates became stricter about awarding new licences, hence some beerhouses closed, whilst others raised their status to become public houses.

The hierarchy of inns and alehouses in Southwell

There was a clear hierarchy of inns and alehouses in Southwell. At the top were the county inns where the local gentry and fashionable social sets frequently met. The Saracen's Head was undoubtedly a county inn. A deed dated 20th October 1396 records the transfer of the building from the archbishop of York to John Fysher and wife, giving evidence that the old inn's illustrious history goes back to medieval times. Dendrochronological analysis of timbers in the north wing suggests a building soon after 1476. Apart from the striking outward appearance of the Saracen's Head, both upstairs and downstairs have spaces that are highly decorated with impressive late Tudor wall paintings. Two probate inventories dating from 1622 and 1683 show how wealthy some of the proprietors were and how fashionable some of the inn's furnishings needed to be to attract the patronage of the upper classes. Linen and pewter were essential items for an inn's reputation, and the inventories show that not only did the Saracen's Head possess these items but also silverware, valuable bedroom furniture and fashionable curtains. The total valuations of the two inventories were £112 and £117 respectively - considerable amounts for the time.

Coaches outside the Saracen's Head Hotel, late 19th century.
(Southwell Civic Society)

Not surprisingly, much interest has always surrounded the historic visit to the Saracen's Head of King Charles I on 5th May 1646 when he was clearly losing the Civil War. The Royalists had suffered a series of setbacks, culminating in their decisive defeat at Naseby. Whilst in Oxford, which was encircled by Parliamentarian troops, he decided to escape and make an agreement with the Scottish Army that was laying siege to the Royalist town of Newark. Charles I employed the French

15th century wall painting in the Saracen's Head Hotel.
(Private Collection)

diplomat Montreuil, resident at the King's Arms (Saracen's Head), to negotiate with the Scots, who Charles expected would be more accommodating than the Parliamentarian army. When Montreuil sent an encouraging message to Charles, he set off from Oxford disguised as a clergyman. The dramatic account of what happened is given by the historian R P Shilton (*The History of Southwell … S & J Ridge, 1818*).

> *On the south side of the gateway, was an apartment, consisting of dining-room, and bed-room. This apartment Montreville [Montreuil] occupied till the king came, when he gave it up to him. The inhabitants still talk of it as the King's Bedchamber. The King sent for the Scotch Commissioners, (who occupied the Palace) before dinner, and dined with them at this inn. Here he gave himself up to them, and in the afternoon, went under escort of their army to Kelham.*

Thus King Charles I spent his last hours of freedom at the Saracen's Head before becoming a prisoner of the Scottish army, who then escorted him northwards and, despite earlier promises, handed him over to the English Parliament in exchange for a waiver of a loan. The two rooms on the ground floor of the hotel, to the left of the arch, which the king used have now been made into one, with a dining area as before and a lounge replacing the bedroom.

The construction of the adjacent Assembly Rooms in 1805 added to the inn's appeal; they subsequently became part of the hotel, now the King Charles dining room (see Chapter 12). The Crown Inn, situated opposite the Saracen's Head, dates back to at least the early 18th century, and was then owned by the Chapter of Southwell Minster.

Victory Parade passing the Saracen's Head Hotel in 1919.
(Private Collection)

Around 1820, when the front of the inn was substantially rebuilt, the Crown aspired to move up the social scale and join its rival as a county inn. Several rooms on the ground floor were available for business meetings and dining. On the first floor there was a 'long room' that was used for sales and assemblies. By the 1830s the Crown had become a successful coaching inn.

Next in the hierarchy were the secondary inns, which, in addition to catering for the needs of the local gentry, had close connections with the wholesale and retail trading of their communities, and, from the 1770s onwards, showed enterprise in running numerous coaching services. Around 1800 there were arguably four town inns, providing accommodation, that fitted this category - the Admiral Rodney, the Cross Keys, the Castle and the Reindeer. The Admiral Rodney, named after the naval hero of the Battle of Cape Vincent, retains an authentic feel from the timber-framed interior of the public bar with its low, original beams. One of the beams is reputed to have come from HMS *Rodney*, whilst another is said to have originated in the bell-ringing gallery at Southwell Minster. On the first floor were a number of bedrooms, providing accommodation for travellers, and a very large ballroom. In the 1940s the ballroom was used as a school by Miss Thomas, a trained dancer, the landlord's daughter. The Cross Keys, situated next to the junction between King Street and Queen Street, was demolished around 1800 for road widening.

The Castle inn was situated on Westgate by the west entrance to the Minster. Like the Cross Keys it was demolished in the early 1800s. In its heyday as a large inn, it provided accommodation for travellers, especially pilgrims and religious groups visiting Southwell Minster. Its demolition leaves us today with an excellent view of Southwell Minster from Westgate. In the 1860s these secondary inns were joined by the recently built Newcastle Arms (now called the Final Whistle) whose interior, yard and outbuildings served the railway, coaching and omnibus businesses that ran between Southwell and Newark.

Further down the hierarchy were the unpretentious carrier inns with stabling, much used by local labourers, wagoners and packmen. They were important bases for the carriage of goods, with yards available for storage and rooms for the carriers to meet their customers. Whereas coaching declined with the coming of the railways, carrying remained an important service until the late 1800s. Foremost amongst these carrier inns were the Black Bull, the Wheatsheaf, the Portland Arms and the White Swan, all of which were situated on the west side of King Street and possessed decent sized yards for horse-drawn transport. Although the Black Bull closed in 1909, the sign for Bull Yard still remains and most of its old outbuildings are now shops. An early deed from 1765 refers to *'dwelling houses, stabling, yards, gardens, backsides, outbuildings with a passage for carter and carriages leading to a yard'*. The White Swan was one of the liveliest of the town inns in the early 1800s, when there were plenty of commercial and recreational activities on the nearby Burgage at Whitsun and at other times of the year. The yards of these four inns, especially the Black Bull and the White Swan, were the location for a wide range of trades such as butchers, blacksmiths, wheelwrights and chandlers, providing innkeepers with valuable rental income.

Next on the social scale were the smaller public houses chiefly situated in Easthorpe and Westhorpe. These 'locals' acted as centres for agricultural labourers, framework knitters and craftsmen who lived in these communities. Good examples are the White Lion (now called the Old Coach House), the Hearty Goodfellow and the George and Dragon (now called the Bramley Apple) in Easthorpe; the Lord Nelson and the Grapes in Westhorpe. Evidence from the *Nottingham Journal*, in a sale notice, shows that the name the 'Hearty Goodfellow' was being used as early as 1817. This 'local' was used in the 18th century as a recruiting centre for the Royal Marines, at a time when the country was at war with France. During the next century its rooms were in regular use for inquests, creditors' meetings, sales and auctions. The Grapes opened as a public house after the 1830 Beerhouse Act, and in the Victorian period many of its regular clientele were agricultural workers and framework knitters from Westhorpe. By the middle of the 1800s most of these smaller public houses had a simple design of a tap room with bar and a smoke room or snug. In the tap room the furniture included deal tables, wooden forms and settles around the walls; the smoke room had slightly better quality furniture and softer seating.

Finally, at the bottom of the hierarchy, there was the large number of alehouses and beerhouses of which little is known. Many were simple domestic dwellings thrown open to the labouring poor to drink in the kitchen or parlour, where they could expect to find a fire, stools, basic tables and chairs and brewing gear. They were the haunt for people who couldn't afford a fire or light in their own rooms. It is likely the Boot and Shoe on the Burgage and the Bear in Westgate fitted this description. There is a notice of the sale of the Boot and Shoe in 1783, when the Burgage was being gentrified by the clearance of cottages and the building of grand houses that now dominate it.

> To be SOLD by Private Contract
> A Small Freehold Estate, situate at Burrage … known by the Sign of the Boot and Shoe, consisting of a Dwelling House, Brewhouse, Coal-house, and Stable, with Yard, Garden and Orchard.

The role of inns in the commercial life of the town

The emergence of the turnpike trusts in the 18th century contributed to the growth of coaching and carrier traffic. Many of the town's inns adapted to cater for the needs of travellers and carriers, providing accommodation, stabling and warehousing. In 1759 the Leadenham to Mansfield turnpike was established, giving commercial traffic easier access to Newark and the Great North Road. The trust also operated a spur as far as Oxton that provided an onward link to Nottingham. Carrier and innkeeper worked in close partnership. It is likely that some Southwell innkeepers themselves conducted a subsidiary carrying business to nearby villages, offering a small parcels service, leaving their wives to look after the inn.

Carrier Robert Morvinson (1857). (Private Collection)

Early in the 19th century, inn-yard paving, stabling and coach house facilities were greatly expanded at the Saracen's Head, the Crown, the Admiral Rodney and later at the Reindeer. Some of the smaller public houses were also determined to be involved, such as the Black Bull,

Stage Coaches at Southwell Inns 1780-1850

Stage Coach	Route	Inns providing service
Accommodation	Birmingham - Newark	Crown, Saracen's Head, Reindeer
Hark Forward	Lincoln - Buxton	Crown
Magna Carta	Nottingham - Lincoln - Hull	Saracen's Head
Champion	Manchester - Lincoln	Crown, Saracen's Head
Celerity	Nottingham - Lincoln - Barton	Crown
Tally Ho	Manchester - Newark	Crown, Saracen's Head
No Wonder	Nottingham - Southwell	Saracen's Head
Royal Mail	Mansfield - Newark	Crown
Standard	Derby - Newark	Admiral Rodney
Queen	Nottingham - Gainsborough	Saracen's Head
Imperial	Nottingham - Hull	Crown
Negotiator	Nottingham - Newark	Admiral Rodney
The Diligence	Nottingham - Lincoln	Not known
New Coach	Derby - Lincoln	Not known
Pilot	Nottingham - Newark	Not known
Omnibus	Mansfield - Southwell	Saracen's Head, Reindeer

which offered the facility to hire a post-chaise. The table on the previous page demonstrates the impact of coach travel on the town inns.

However, from the 1840s onwards the arrival of the railway signalled the beginning of the end of the great coaching age. Wherever a line was opened, the immediate result was the cessation of local coach services, which could not compete with regard to speed, comfort, cost or capacity.

Local inns and their innkeepers also had very strong commercial ties with the malting industry, which after agriculture and textiles was possibly the most important industry in Southwell in the 18th and 19th centuries. Trade directories show that there were as many as eight maltsters operating in the mid-19th century, though by the 1890s the malting trade in the town was in decline due to the strong competition from the large malthouses in Newark and Mansfield. Inevitably, there were close commercial links between the inns and the two town breweries, which were established later in the 19th century - Westgate Brewery (1876) and Southwell Brewery Company (1880). This continues with the growth in popularity of local micro-breweries.

Over the last century there has been a decline in the use of local inns for commercial purposes and the number of hostelries has reduced to nine (2016). However, a larger proportion of public houses now offer food, and there is still a demand for function rooms for meetings, weddings and private parties. Thus, whilst far fewer in number, the public houses of Southwell continue to play a significant social and commercial role in the life of the town.

Chapter 11

Southwell's Industry

Peter Lyth

With its famous Minster and important ecclesiastical status, Southwell does not seem like a town with an industrial past. As an ancient market centre Southwell had the usual associated activities such as watermills, windmills, and skilled crafts such as smiths, wheelwrights and coopers. A careful inspection of the historical record shows that in the 18th and early 19th centuries the town also had significant textile industries and trades associated with brewing. According to the Tithe Commutation Award, in 1840 Southwell had no fewer than 65 framework knitters' workshops, 8 malt and hop kilns, 2 cotton mills, a tannery and a hat factory.[1] After the coming of the railways, however, the town's comparatively small-scale industries began to decline. This did not apply to lace making that came to the town in the latter part of the 19th century, and at its peak employed around 150, many of them highly skilled.

This chapter looks at Southwell's industry, focusing mainly on the years between 1700 and 1950, during which time the town's population rose from under 1,000 to over 3,500. The illustrations should encourage the curious visitor to see a number of the buildings still standing - now residential homes, but once a hive of industry.

Spinning, weaving, knitting and lace making

There were weavers and knitters in Southwell from the Tudor period and in 1683 the Saracen's Head Hotel included a 'Dyers' Room'; dyers being the labour aristocracy of the textile trade and prominent enough to have their own room at the town's foremost county inn. Weaving grew in prosperity and importance during the 18th century when Southwell's weavers were served by up to four local cotton mills. By 1792 they were demanding a rise in their wages of *'an extra halfpenny a yard for weaving plain linens, etc., etc. and a penny a yard for ticking, common table linen, woollens etc. and in proportion for figured work'*. Clearly framework knitting was a thriving industry, particularly for hosiery and knitwear, and by the early years of the 19th century was *'the dominant textile industry in the region'*.[2]

Maythorne Mill, built in 1785 to produce cotton for Southwell's knitters. (Peter Lyth)

Cotton spinning developed a little later, concentrated in early 'proto-factories' built on the plan perfected by the Lancashire entrepreneur and inventor Richard Arkwright, who had moved to Nottingham to build his first spinning factory. Before steam power, there was a rush to get good sites for cotton mills close to fast flowing rivers and the River Greet was such a river. By 1785 Thomas Caunt & Co had a cotton mill, built on the Arkwright model, at the small hamlet of Maythorne on the northern border of the parish. Along with the mill were several cottages for workers, a warehouse and a reservoir on the Greet to serve the water wheel. The cotton it produced supplied Southwell's framework knitters and the stocking trade.[3]

At this time, in the early years of the industrial revolution, cotton production expanded dramatically from being a small-scale domestic undertaking into Britain's most vibrant industry. A series of key inventions led to the mechanization of textile production and an enormous increase in productivity. These inventions reduced the need for direct manual operation and prepared the way for mill production and steam power in the 19th century. Little Southwell played a small part in the early cotton revolution, but it didn't last. The Maythorne mill couldn't compete with the more advanced mule technology used in Lancashire cotton mills, and in the early 19th century it switched from cotton to silk production, supplying the Nottingham lace industry. With Nottingham rapidly becoming a major centre of lace production, this was probably a smart move. The silk mill at Maythorne continued in operation until the Second World War, with water power delivering 16 horsepower and operating 2,200 spindles. In 1838 there were 70 employees at Maythorne mill, mainly women. A darker side of the trade is illustrated by the fact that in 1841, 10-year-old girls were working at the Maythorne silk mill.[4]

Elsewhere in Southwell, lace was produced at the former House of Correction, on the north-eastern corner of the Burgage (see Chapter 8). There is some irony in the fact that a Victorian factory was established in a former prison; whether or not workers had occasion to feel like 'inmates', we do not know.

Lace was initially manufactured by W A Gregory from 1885 until 1895 when it was taken over by Careys of Nottingham. They continued in business, producing 'Nottingham lace', until 1956. The cotton yarn came from Manchester and the finished lace was then sent to Nottingham to be made up into curtains. During the Second World War they manufactured camouflage netting. Power came from a steam

*The 1867 wing of the House of Correction used by Carey's
for lace curtain making.
(Courtesy of J Harlow)*

engine driving shafts and pulleys to the 57 lace machines, which were controlled by an early form of punch card, known as the Jacquard system.[5] After the factory closed, the site was taken over by Rainbow Night Freight Ltd, who operated there until 2014. The site is now residential housing, with two sections of the original buildings retained for conversion.

The Malthouse on Lower Kirklington Road, built in 1825 by the miller Charles Walker, now stylish cottages.
(Mike Kirton)

Hops and malt

Industry and agriculture were in many ways complementary until the 19th century and the best examples in Southwell were the industries associated with brewing: hop growing and malting. Writing in the mid-18th century, the agricultural historian Robert Lowe estimated that there were about 200 acres devoted to hop growing in Southwell. Hops were an important crop on the clay land of north Nottinghamshire; known as 'North Clay' hops, they were much stronger than Kentish hops and, according to Lowe, this led people who were, *'accustomed to the latter* (i.e. Kentish hops) *to object to their flavour as rank'*.[6] Hop growing was well established on both sides of the River Greet between Norwood Park and Normanton, and reminders of this can be found in place names such as Hopkiln Lane, linking Kirklington Road with Halam Road, and Hopyard on Lower Kirklington Road. Hops fetched a good price too: the

The former Ideal Cinema in Westgate: once the site of a brewery, then a cinema in the 1930s and more recently part of a residential development. (Peter Lyth)

lawyer George Hodgkinson records in his diary that on 6th July 1770 he *sold Mr Biggs a bag of hops* (over a hundredweight or 50 kg) *for £9.00*.[7] That was a lot of money in 1770.

Malting is the process whereby grain (usually barley) is partially germinated by soaking it in water and then dried in hot air. The result of this age-old process is malted grain, which has its starch changed to maltose sugar and is ready to play a vital role in the production of beer. In the early part of the 19th century malting was the most important industry after textiles. Maltsters were often prosperous farmers, millers or, indeed, brewers. In the 1860s the number of malthouses declined, like other local Southwell industries, which had difficulty facing competition from larger producers after the arrival of the railways.

Small-scale local brewers were common in Britain at this time and Southwell had its share of local pubs and alehouses, which brewed their

Early 20th century photograph of the level crossing on Station Road, with the station on the left and the Newcastle Arms on the right.
(Britain in Old Photographs - Southwell)

The level crossing as it is today with the Final Whistle on the right. Access to the Southwell Trail is from both sides.
(Peter Lyth)

own beer (Chapter 10). They succumbed in the later 19th century to competition from the bigger Newark brewers, such as Warwick & Richardson, although Southwell did retain one brewer at the Westgate Brewery owned by Marston, Thompson & Evershed. By the time of its final closure in the 1920s it was probably used only as a distribution centre for Southwell's pubs, but remains interesting for the fact that it represents an example of the change taking place in Britain's entertainment industry in the 20th century when it was rebuilt in 1932 as the 'Ideal Cinema'. A place for making beer became a place for making dreams come true as Southwell's citizens were introduced to the stars of Hollywood.

The railway age

In 1844 the Midland Railway was formed in Derby out of the union of three competing companies and a powerful new transport system began to spread through the Trent valley. In 1847 the Midland opened a branch line from Rolleston Junction, on the Nottingham-Lincoln line, to Southwell. The line was re-launched in 1860, with a new Southwell station, and in 1871 a western extension to Mansfield was completed. The line soon became a busy freight link for coal from Mansfield and agricultural produce from the neighbourhood, especially milk and grain. Thus the town's local industries, which had thrived a century before, began to face more direct competition from larger producers in Newark, Mansfield and Nottingham and many began to go under.

Passenger traffic was always thin on the Southwell-Mansfield stretch of the line and the services were discontinued in 1929, with exception made for the occasional Southwell Racecourse Special bringing punters from Mansfield to the racetrack at Rolleston (see Chapter 12). The line in the opposite direction remained open, however, until 1959; a vibrant passenger service known affectionately as the 'Southwell Paddy' - making up to 16 daily return trips from Southwell to Rolleston Junction - and consisting of an elderly tank engine pulling a single carriage. In the 1960s the line was run for a few years as a coal line before the track was finally lifted and Southwell's old railway reborn as a much-loved nature trail.[8] Today, all that remains of the old station is the stationmaster's house and the station pub, the 'Newcastle Arms', which was built to serve passengers and has since been re-named, appropriately enough, the 'Final Whistle'.

The River Greet provided power to industry in Southwell not only at Maythorne but also where the road to Normanton crosses the river; indeed it seems likely that a corn mill has been on that site for up to 1,000 years. In 1851 the Caudwell family bought and expanded the mill with local wheat being brought in by road and, after the opening of the Midland Railway link from Rolleston, by rail (Caudwell's had their own railway siding adjacent to Southwell station). Not only local corn but also imported wheat from Australia, Argentina and Canada arrived at Caudwell's Mill, a lot of it coming by barge up the Trent from Hull to a wharf at Fiskerton. Their prize-winning *Greet Lily Flour* was produced by generations of Caudwells up until the mill was finally closed in 1969. Fire is always a risk at corn grinding mills and Caudwell's suffered three fires between 1867 and 1917, on each occasion taking the opportunity to modernize the plant. The landmark water tower was added after the fire of 1893.[9]

Besides the Caudwells, perhaps the most impressive industrialist to live in Southwell was the Nottingham factory owner and textile magnate William Norton Hicking. In 1889 he bought Brackenhurst, a house built in the 1830s by a local vicar on the Nottingham Road, and during the next 30 years he proceeded to turn it into an imposing stately home and garden known as Brackenhurst Hall.[10] Typical of many rich businessmen of the late Victorian period, Hicking's purpose - despite his lowly origins (he was the son of a stationmaster from Eastwood) - was to become a country gentleman. Through a major programme of modifications, enlargements and embellishments, he created a lavish residence complete with bell tower, ancient oak panelling, an Italianate rose garden, a 'dew pond' and a 'ha-ha', to keep his prize shorthorn cattle from wandering onto the Hall's lawns and terraces. In 1917 Hicking handed over Brackenhurst Hall to the War Office for use as a military hospital. In 1915 another property he owned, Burgage Manor, had become a military hospital. He was rewarded with a knighthood in 1919. When he died in 1947, Brackenhurst was sold to Nottinghamshire

Top: *Caudwell's Mill in the 1930s.*
(Britain in Old Photographs - Southwell)
Below: *The Mill has since been converted to apartments.*
(Peter Lyth)

Brackenhurst Hall as it is today.
(Mike Kirton)

County Council and re-opened two years later as an agricultural college with 27 students and the author's father, Philip Lyth, as its first principal. In 1999 it became part of Nottingham Trent University, which has expanded the teaching facilities on the north side of the Hall as well as developing the popular equestrian section at nearby Brackenhurst Farm.

With the general movement from manufacturing to a service and leisure economy towards the end of the 20th century, Southwell began to develop its tourism industry. In the 1990s the Minster, the National Trust site at the Workhouse (Chapter 9) and the site of the original 'Bramley Apple' all became icons of the burgeoning heritage industry. Blue plaques appeared on the walls of the town explaining its history to its citizens and visitors. The industries that had supported brewing and textile production a century earlier, became objects of fascination for the heritage tourist, now a major source of income for the town's traders.

[1] Reproduced in Stanley Chapman, 'The Rise and Decline of Local Industries, c. 1600-1850', in S D Chapman and Derek Walker (eds), *Southwell: The Town and its People, Vol. II*, (Southwell: Southwell Local History Society, 2006), p. 66.
[2] Chapman, 'The Rise and Decline ...', p. 68.
[3] Peter L O'Malley, 'Southwell - its trade and industry', in *Southwell: The Town and its People, An Historical Survey by Local Writers* (Southwell: Southwell Local History Society, 1995), pp. 39-42.
[4] Margaret Ashworth, 'Southwell - its trade and industry', pp. 53-4.
[5] David Hutchinson, 'Southwell - its trade and industry', p. 54 and Rob Smith, *Nottinghamshire House of Correction, Southwell (1611-1880)* (Southwell: Southwell Local History Society, 2015), pp. 51-2.
[6] Philip Lyth, *A History of Nottinghamshire Farming* (Newark: Cromwell Press, 1989), p. 30.
[7] Robert Hardstaff & Philip Lyth, *Georgian Southwell, The Journals of the George Hodgkinsons, 1770-81* (Newark: Newark & Sherwood District Council, 1990), p. 54.
[8] Derek Walker, 'A Miscellany', in *Southwell: The Town and its People*, pp. 169-70.
[9] Margaret Ashworth, 'Southwell - its trade and industry', in *Southwell: The Town and its People*, p. 57.
[10] Brackenhurst was the birthplace in 1861 of the distinguished First World War general, Field Marshal Edmund Allenby, after whom a street in Southwell is named (see Chapter 12).

Acknowledgement: Virginia Carpenter et al., *Britain in Old Photographs - Southwell* (Stroud: Sutton Publishing, 1996).

Chapter 12

In and Around the Town

Michael J Kirton

The Assembly Rooms

The majority of towns had assembly rooms and a few have survived, either as meeting rooms or in name only, having been put to alternative use. The Southwell assembly rooms are now incorporated into the Saracen's Head Hotel, but the original façade remains.

*The Assembly Rooms.
(Mike Kirton)*

Assembly rooms were, as the name suggests, places where townspeople got together for various functions. Typically, they were meeting rooms for the middle classes where, in season, regular assemblies and dances took place. The dances were opportunities for young middle-class ladies to meet their future husbands. Well brought-up young ladies, particularly in the Georgian period, were taught the finer arts of housekeeping and trained to dance so that they could impress at the assembly. Many assemblies were organised by professionals who were known as 'kings' and 'queens'. As well as catering for dancing, all good assembly rooms had facilities for card players.

Up until 1805 Southwell assemblies had taken place in the Crown Hotel. However, at this time a group of the town's well-to-do subscribed to the building of the Assembly Rooms that were designed in classical style by the famous local architect Richard Ingleman. Well-known characters, such as the Bechers and the Hodgkinsons, were trustees and administrators of the enterprise. The building had several uses, with the lower floors used as a court room for petty sessions, a news room, and two rooms let to the hotel. The upper floor was a well-appointed assembly room. The Southwell assemblies were patronised from a wide area. At some stage when assemblies went out of vogue, the whole building was incorporated into the Saracen's Head Hotel.

The Burgage War Memorial

As the First World War was coming to an end, the people of Southwell were debating how their war dead should be honoured and what support should be given to the returning troops, many of whom could be in need of help. A committee was appointed and it was their recommendation that a memorial hall be commissioned along with cottage homes and a memorial cross. The estimated cost for this ambitious project was around £5,000. Sadly, by September 1919 the total raised was only £466. 19s 0d, which was just sufficient to build the cross we see today on Burgage Green. It was dedicated on Saturday 30th April 1921. The enthusiasm for the original plan had dimmed as post-war austerity began to bite.

Dedication of the War Memorial on the Burgage 21st April 1921 - A J Loughton Collection. (By kind permission of the Dean and Chapter)

The war had been costly to Southwell. Out of a population of approximately 3,200, during the period 1914-19, around 650 men served in the armed forces, but 108 of them did not return. This figure of almost 17% was well above the British average of 10% and more on a par with the French losses. One reason for this high figure is that the local territorial company, the 'Southwell Pals', part of the 8th Battalion, Sherwood Foresters, were in front line action from March/April 1915 for the duration of the war. They suffered heavy casualties, particularly in 1915, when 7 men died in one night at the Battle of Hohenzollern. A full list of the war dead is displayed on a roll of honour in the transept of the Minster, together with the 24 who died in the Second World War. On the gatehouse to the House of Correction is a memorial tablet to the 16 men of Careys, the lace makers, who perished in the First World War, many of them were members of the territorial company.

Following the Second World War the War Memorial Park, with access from Bishops' Drive, was dedicated. It is on land that was part of the Archbishop's Deer Park and is now used for sporting activities.

The Old Theatre

Tucked away in the corner of the (former) Market Place, at the junction of King Street and Queen Street, is Southwell's Georgian Theatre. It is now part of the 'Old Theatre Deli'. If you are visiting the 'Deli' for refreshments and the first floor is open, you must take the opportunity of viewing the restored theatre. Prior to the theatre's opening in 1812 dramatic performances took place in large private houses around the Minster and the Burgage. Lord Byron is said to have performed at Burgage House during his period in Southwell between 1803 and 1809. Before becoming a theatre, the building had been used as a depot for the arms of the Southwell Regiment of Local Militia.

In 1812 Joseph Smedley, the leader of a travelling theatre group, was granted a licence to perform in Southwell for 40 days. Family records reveal that the Smedley group, including members of his large family, together with his successors visited Southwell for a summer season every other year until 1845. The Smedleys put on a variety of popular productions and Southwell was part of a circuit that covered a wide area from Cambridgeshire to Lincolnshire, across to Nottinghamshire and Derbyshire, and north to Yorkshire. By the 1820s the Smedleys appear to have been quite successful and established ownership or had shares in some of the venues, including Sleaford, March, Howden, Selby and Wakefield. A number of playbills advertise that the productions were 'domestic comedies'. Titles such as *A Way to Get Married*, *A Batchelor's Miseries,* and *The Haunted House* are amongst the many productions. The plays in Southwell seem to have been well patronised, with the Smedley's accounts showing receipts of £138 6s 0d in 1812, which compared favourably with seasons in Belper, Oakham, Ripley, and Wirksworth. The accounts also detail a list of locals and organisations who bought tickets in advance. This suggests a middle-class audience, although tickets were also sold at the door. There is no evidence to suggest that the behaviour of local audiences matched the 'raucous' behaviour reported in London theatres in this period. By 1845 the regular seasons seem to have disappeared, although there is some evidence of amateur theatre groups using the facility until the early 20th Century. In 1904 a photograph records a production by

Southwell Theatre Group. Additionally, local theatre groups used the facilities for rehearsals until the 1960s.

With the passing of the regular visiting players the building was inherited by the Loughton family in 1881. The well-known local photographer Alfred Loughton lived at the premises until his death in 1953. Alfred was a very accomplished man whose skills extended to metalwork, violin making, gas fitting and bell hanging. He also invented the 'Southwell Cycle'. In 1930 Alfred photographed George Bernard Shaw outside the Old Theatre.

In recent years the premises have been used as a saleroom and were finally brought back to life by the Tinley family when they converted the premises to the 'Old Theatre Deli', where local organisations occasionally put on performances.

Alfred Loughton at work.
(Private Collection)

George Bernard Shaw photographed in 1930 by Alfred Loughton at the entrance to the Old Theatre.
(Private Collection)

(Adapted from an article by Roger Dobson)

Easthorpe

Easthorpe, now an integral part of Southwell, was for centuries a village community in its own right. The serious explorer is advised to pick up a copy of the Easthorpe Heritage Trail (No. 4) from the Tourist Information Centre in Minster Chambers, Church Street.

Travelling from Newark-on-Trent the view as you turn the corner at the Old Coach House with the Minster in the background is impressive with many 18th century, and earlier, buildings on both sides of the road. Until the 19th century there were a number of farms and trade workshops centred on agriculture. In addition, there were other local industries such as framework knitting and malting. The industries have disappeared, leaving an interesting collection of three storeyed Georgian, and older, buildings that are worth a look. There are two large 'country' houses along Easthorpe. On the corner of Fiskerton Road stands Easthorpe House and nearby is Easthorpe Lodge, which is best seen from a public footpath running from Farthingate Close. The lodge

*A view along Easthorpe showing the Hearty Goodfellow.
(Mike Kirton)*

is an 1812 extension of a 17th century farmhouse, the home of the Caudwell family who owned the flour mill at the bottom of Station Road, straggling the River Greet (now apartments). Away from the bustle of the main street is a pleasant footpath known as Shady Lane, running from the side of the Hearty Goodfellow public house. The lane bridges the Potwell Dyke and by the bridge are the remains of a small water-powered mill, sadly only evidence of the foundations is visible. On the other side of the public house is a private garden that is the home of the original Bramley Apple tree.

The Original Bramley Apple tree.
(By kind permission of Roger Merryweather)

The Bramley apple has a fascinating history. In the early 19th century a girl called Mary Ann Brailsford planted some pips from an apple grown on a tree at the bottom of her garden. Remarkably, one produced a seedling and in 1837 it bore fruit. Eventually the garden came into the hands of Matthew Bramley who continued to enjoy the fruit. In 1856 Henry Merryweather, the son of a local nurseryman, came across the apple and was allowed to take cuttings with the variety being named after Matthew Bramley. The apple was exhibited before the Royal Horticultural Society in 1876 and by 1883 was shown at the National Apple Congress and awarded a First Class Certificate. Whilst the original tree has survived to the present day, it is in need of expert attention and has been cloned by staff at the University of Nottingham. The Merryweather Nursery had an international reputation and the Bramley apple is world famous with a serious group of devotees in Japan who visit from time to time.

A further claim to fame in Easthorpe is the site of the South Well, which is on the junction of Fiskerton Road and Crink Lane (see picture on page 2). It is said to be the site of the spring where the 7th century Archbishop of York, Paulinus, baptised local people when he visited Southwell. If you feel energetic, apart from the walk mentioned in the Easthorpe Heritage Trail, walk along Crink Lane, and as the land rises you can glimpse some wonderful views of the Minster and the town. The walk will eventually bring you out at the other end of the town near the new Minster School, and from there a healthy walk via Brackenhurst Hall (Chapter 11) brings you to the settlement of Westhorpe.

Westhorpe

The hamlet of Westhorpe has a tranquil setting, by-passed by the Oxton Road that leads on to Nottingham. Its present atmosphere only hints of a time when this was a busy working community. Many of the buildings are old farmsteads and the cottages as you enter Westhorpe housed framework knitters. The industries have long gone and the hamlet is a pleasant residential area, home to a number of local artists. The Westhorpe Dumble winds its way through the area and the Southwell Tourism Partnership have produced a trail guide, 'The Westhorpe Dumble' (No. 5), which is well worth obtaining so that you can explore the hamlet in more detail.

The quietness of 21st century Westhorpe hides the struggle to earn a living by villagers toiling sixteen hours a day on their mechanical knitting frames. Back in 1844 it was recorded that there were 120 frames located here. Nottinghamshire has a sad history of distressed framework knitters, with riots in Nottingham as they campaigned for fairer wages. The 1851 Census listed around 100 framework knitters in Southwell of which 75 were still working, including 8 listed as 'Pauper Framework Knitters'. Over the years the local cottage industry declined as steam power in larger factories took over from human-powered machines.

A view of Westhorpe showing the former workmen's cottages. The Workman's Rest Institute was on the left at the end of the row of cottages.
(Mike Kirton)

The other local industry was agriculture, which had its many peaks and troughs over the years. Along the road through the hamlet there is much evidence of agricultural buildings, with some cottagers keeping a few animals to feed themselves. Most of these buildings are now converted to domestic use. To support the local industries, there was a blacksmith, a joinery shop and a lodging house for passing tramps. Westhorpe, therefore, had a very mixed economy with some families working hard for very little return. Concern for their welfare prompted Mrs Warrand of Westhorpe Hall to open the Workman's Rest Institute for the benefit of working men in their leisure hours. The building is at the western end of the row of cottages to the south of Sunnyside.

Sunnyside terrace was originally sixteen back-to-back houses, subsequently converted to eight by taking out the rear walls, and then reduced to five to facilitate the widening of the Oxton Road. In front of Sunnyside there was once a market area.

Sunnyside terrace at the entrance to Westhorpe.
(Mike Kirton)

Field Marshall Viscount Allenby.
(Private Collection)

Opposite Sunnyside is Allenby Road, named after Field Marshall Viscount Allenby. He was born at Brackenhurst Hall (see Chapter 11) on 23rd April 1861 whilst his mother was visiting her parents, the Reverend and Mrs Thomas Coates Caine. Viscount Allenby served with distinction in the First World War and led British troops into Jerusalem when it was liberated on 11th December 1917. One of the regiments serving under his command was the South Notts Hussars with senior officers from this area.

The 'big house' is Westhorpe Hall, rebuilt in 1820, now converted into apartments, and

Westhorpe Hall.
(Antony Woolley)

formerly the home of the Warrand family and then through marriage to the Hanmers, the owners of the Westhorpe estate. Group Captain Hanmer, DFC, was a breeder of racehorses and these were stabled at Hall Farm on the Westhorpe estate. Prior to the Warrand family the principal family was the Clays, whose lineage has been traced back to the 14th century. William Clay, who died in 1692, was the archbishop of York's steward in Southwell.

Situated by the side of the Dumble at the west end of Westhorpe is St Catherine's Well, which was said to have healing powers. This is one of four holy wells in Southwell. Easthorpe's 'South Well' has already been mentioned. According to Shilton, the historian, the other two were the Lord's Well and the Lady's Well at the Minster. In 1481 the archbishop of York granted a licence for the building of a chapel in honour of St Catherine the Virgin. The chapel is long gone and there is a private dwelling on the site.

A stroll through Westhorpe is to be recommended and occasionally you could be drawn in to one of the artist's homes when they organise 'Studio Open Days'.

Southwell Racecourse.
(Private Collection)

Southwell Racecourse

Horse racing has taken place in Southwell for many years, and the origins are thought to go back to a time when tenants of the Archbishop's Liberty were obliged to come into town on a particular day to pay their rents. The day became a local holiday with various activities including horse racing on the Burgage. Many of the tenants rode into town and raced their own horses, no doubt for small wagers.

By 1883 racing had become an organised event with prize money up to £30 on offer, with races being held on the Thursday after Whitsun. The Burgage became too small a venue, and in 1886 a limited company was formed and a much larger course was constructed running parallel to Lower Kirklington Road for about three quarters of a mile and circling back, crossing the Ropewalk. This included a grandstand and four years later a further stand was constructed and racing was extended to two days, with an extra day in October. Racing continued on this course until October 1897 when the National Hunt refused to extend its licence.

On 11th May 1898 the Southwell Racecourse Company Ltd was formed and racing was moved to land at Rolleston, where it continues to the present day. Apart from a suspension in the Second World War, the number of race meetings steadily grew. In 1989 a large investment was made in an all-weather course, one of only a handful in the country. 'Racing from Southwell' is now a regular feature on the sporting calendar.

Recent Publications by Southwell & District Local History Society

This society has, over the years, published a number of books about the town and its people. The following is a list of the more recent books:

Southwell at War, 1914-1919, Michael Austin, Michael J Kirton and Lance Wright (2014)
During the period of the Great War at least 650 men from the town served their country and a high proportion, 108, died on the battlefields of Europe and the Middle East. This well-researched book contains biographical details of these men and many stories of their exploits and sacrifice. Extracts from the *Newark Advertiser* chronicle the news stories from the period.

Southwell & District at War, 1939-45, Roger Dobson
Edited by Michael J Kirton
Volume 1, Keep Smiling Through, (2015)
Volume 2, We'll Meet Again, (2016)
These unique volumes have captured memories from people in the district who lived through the Second World War. Their memories are vivid and many of the accounts from the various theatres of war are both dramatic and heart rending. The stories from the Home Front form a large part of these two volumes and chronicle how those left at home coped with the shortages and fundraising, whilst waiting for the return of their loved ones.

Nottinghamshire House of Correction, Southwell, 1611-1880, Rob Smith (2015)
A summary of the history of the first house of correction and its subsequent rebuilding in the early 19th century. Rob Smith has undertaken extensive research into the design of the prison and its replication in other parts of the world.

Southwell Settlers, Doris Stirk, with a forward by Rob Smith (2015)
A history of the town of Southwell in South Africa founded in 1820 by a group of settlers from this area. It is a little-known story of emigration from the UK in 1820.

It's Not What You Know ... Patronage in Eighteenth and Nineteenth Century Nottinghamshire, Edited by Richard Gaunt (2012)
A collection of essays by Austin, Chapman, Gaunt and Kirton, based on lectures given at a Nottinghamshire Local History Society Day School in Spring 2011.

Georgian Diary, 1780, Michael J Kirton (2011)
Georgian Diary, 1781, Robert E Hardstaff (2000)
These two books offer a fascinating insight into life in 18th century Southwell, and beyond, through the eyes of a young apprentice attorney, working in the town and heavily involved in the administration of the Peculiar of Southwell. The transcribed diaries are supported by explanatory essays of the life and times, including news from the American War of Independence.

Minster People, Edited by Stanley Chapman and Derek Walker (2009)
A collection of well-researched essays on people whose lives impinged on the Minster, men and women, from medieval days to recent times.

Southwell The Town and Its People, Volume II
Edited by Stanley Chapman and Derek Walker (2006)
An in-depth look by a team of researchers into the industries and people who shaped this historic town.

Visit Southwell & District Local History Society at: www.southwellhistorysociety.co.uk for more information.

Index - People

Adams, William	69	Fogg, John	84-5
Alfred the Great	14		
Allenby, Field Marshall Viscount	120	George III, King	48
		Gerard, Archbishop	25
Aragon, Catherine of	23	Godson, Sara	84
Arkwright, Richard	55, 100-1		
		Hall, Cecil	61
Ball, Peter	17	Hanmer, Gp Capt., DFC	121
Barre, John	28	Heathcote, Catherine	56-7, 65
Barritt, Mary	50	Henry VIII, King	18, 23, 46, 67
Barrow, Revd	56	Hicking, William N	107
Becher, John Jnr	6	Hodgkinson, George	5, 112
Becher, John Snr	6	Holden, Isaac	75
Becher, Revd J T	6, 47, 54, 56, 61, 63, 70-1, 74-5, 78-9, 112	Hood, Robin	21
		Howard, John	68-9
		Hutchinson, Benjamin	74-5
Boyce, Frances	64	Hykeling, Henry de	27
Brailsford, Mary Ann	117		
Bramley, Matthew	117	Ingleman, Richard	61, 70, 72
Byron, Catherine G	62, 64		
Byron, Lord George	6, 61-4, 75, 114	Jackson, Magnus	28
		James I, King	23, 68
Caudwell family	107, 117		
Charles I, King	5, 23, 91-3	Knight, Henry Gally	21
Clare, Earl of	64		
Clay, William	121	Lampart, Sarah	64
Cromwell, Oliver	29, 35	Leacroft, Capt. John	63
		Leacroft, Julia	63
David, King	18	Loughton, Alfred	115
Defoe, Daniel	ix	Lowe family	65
Denison, George	38	Lyth, Philip	109
Dickinson, William	7, 14		
		Matthews, Reginald	32
Eadwig, or Edwy, King	15, 27	Merryweather, Henry	117-18
Eccles, G S	32	Michael, Archangel	18
Edward II, King	23	Mole, Matthew	74-5
Elizabeth I, Queen	23, 46, 67-8, 77	Mompesson, Revd W	44, 47
		Montreuil (Diplomat)	92
Falkner, Evelyn	61-2	Moore, Henry	29

Morvinson, Robert	96		Standley, Henry	75
Mynheer, Nicholas	21-2		Sumner, William	83
			Sutton, Sir Richard	5
Neepe, William	50-2, 54			
Neild, James	70		Thomas, II	15
			Thomas, Miss	94
Oskytel, Archbishop	2, 7, 15		Thompson, Robert	21
			Turner, J M W, RA	21
Paulinus, Archbishop	1, 118			
Pigot, Elizabeth	62-3		Wade, John	56
Pigot, John	62		Walker, Charles	65, 89, 103
Pulford, Stephen	36		Warrand, Mrs	119
			Weightman, Mary	82
Reyntiens, Patrick	17		Weightman, Thomas	82
Richardson, Maria	83		Wesley, John	49, 52, 57
Ridding, Bishop			Wilkins,	
Dr George	21		Archdeacon George	56-7
			Williams, Mary	55
Shaw, George Bernard	115		Wolsey, Cardinal	23
Smedley, Joseph	114		Wright, John	30, 32
Smith, Basil Rushby	32		Wright, Revd J S	31
St Thomas the Martyr	61		Wylde, John Charles	57

Index - General

Ad Pontem, East Stoke	7	Cranfield House	44-5, 48
Admiral Rodney PH	89, 94, 96-7	Cross Keys PH	89, 94
Anglo-Saxon church	1, 7, 13-14	Crown Inn	87, 89, 93, 96-7
Anti-pauper system	79	Cupid	22
Archbishop's Palace	2, 3, 5, 7, 23-6		
Arkwright mills	55, 101	Diet, Workhouse	81-2
Assembly Rooms	6, 93, 111-12	Domesday Book	23
		Dunham Prebend	45
Baptist Church	33, 53-5		
Bear P H	89, 95	Easthorpe Endowed School	30
Beckingham Prebend	42	Easthorpe	116-18
Beer Act 1830	90, 95	Easthorpe Hall	30
Bishop's Palace	26	Easthorpe House	116
Black Bull Inn	89, 94-5	Easthorpe Lodge	116
Black Horse PH	89, 96	Eaton Prebend	42
Board schools	33	Edgehill House	14, 42
Boot and Shoe PH	89, 95-6	Education Act 1870	33
Brackenhurst Hall	107-8, 118, 120	Education Act 1902	32
Bramley apple	109, 117-18	Education Act 1944	32
Bramley Apple PH	89, 95	Education garden	25-6
Bridewell	67	Edward Cludd School	35-7
Burgage House	63	Eleven plus	33
Burgage Manor	60, 62-5	Elmfield House	56, 65-6
Burgage Manor Court	61	Enclosure Acts	5
Burgage, The	59-66	Evangelical Revival	54
Bury St Edmonds Goal	70		
		Final Whistle PH	89, 94
Carey & Sons Ltd	5, 76, 101-2, 113	Firbeck House	85-6
Castle Inn	89, 94	First World War	5-6, 22, 32, 64, 76, 107, 112-3, 120
Caudwell House	86		
Chantry priests	30		
Chantry Priest House	28-9	Flint tools	7
Chapter of canons	3, 16	Framework knitting	5, 55, 73, 95, 100-1, 116, 118-9
Chedworth	12		
Christus Rex	17		
Civil War	5, 17, 23, 28-9		
Cock fighting	87, 90	Fugitive Pieces	63
Commonwealth, The	46		
County Coroners	3	Gloucester Penitentiary	71-2

Governor's house	65	Junior Department	33
Grapes, The, PH	89, 95	Lady's Well	121
Gregory, W A	101	Leverton Prebend	42
Guardian's Minutes	84	Livestock sales	60
Halloughton Prebend	42	Local Education	
Harvey's Field	10-11	Authority	32
Hearty Goodfellow PH	89, 95	Local militia	114
Heritage Lottery Fund	2, 23	Lord's Well	121
Holy Trinity Church	49, 51, 55-8		
Hops	5, 103-4	Maltings	65, 87, 89, 98
Horse racing	87	Marston, Thompson	
House of Correction	5-6, 63-5, 67-76, 101, 113	& Evershed	106
		Master's punishment book	84
Ideal Cinema	104, 106	Maythorne Mill	100-1, 107
Industrial Revolution	54-5	Merryweather's Nursery	118
Industry	99-110	Methodist Church	49-53
Inns and Alehouses Map	88	Midland Railway	106
Inns and Alehouses:		Millbank Prison	71
Admiral Rodney	89, 94, 96-7	Minster	1-3, 5-9, 11, 13, 15, 26-30,33, 35, 38-41, 45-6, 49-50, 54-7, 66, 78, 87, 93-4, 99, 109, 113-14, 116, 118, 121
Bear	89, 95		
Black Bull Inn	89, 94-5		
Black Horse	89, 96		
Boot and Shoe	89, 95-6		
Bramley Apple	89, 95		
Castle Inn	89, 94		
Cross Keys	89, 94	Angel window	17
Crown Inn	87, 89, 93, 96-7	Bread pews	22
Final Whistle PH	89, 94	Candle Chapel	21
Grapes, The , PH	89, 95	Chapter House	18-19, 21
Hearty Goodfellow PH	89, 95	Christus Rex	17
Newcastle Arms	89, 94	Cupid	9, 22
Old Coach House PH	116	Font	17
Portland Arms	89, 94	High Altar	20-1
Red Lion PH	89	Norman nave	16-17
Reindeer Inn	89, 94, 96-7	Pilgrims' Chapel	18
Saracen's Head Hotel	5-6, 42, 49, 89-93, 96-7, 99, 111-2	Pulpitum	18
		Residence, The	8-9, 14, 26, 47-8
		Tympanum	17-18
Wheatsheaf PH	89, 94	Vicars' Court	8, 26
White Lion PH	89, 95	Minster Lodge	42
White Swan PH	87, 89, 94-5	Minster School	6, 15, 27-38
Iron Age	7	Minster View	85-6

Mompesson House, Salisbury	44	Peculiar of Southwell	3	
		Pentecostals	49	
		Police Station	65	
Naseby, Battle of	91	Pony races	60	
National Apple Congress	118	Poor Law Amendment Act 1834	79, 82	
National Health System	86	Poor Laws	6, 77, 79, 85-6	
National School	33-4	Poor Law Board	84	
National Trust	86	Population	6	
NatWest Bank	42	Portland Arms	89, 94	
Newark & Sherwood District Council	3	Prebendal houses	1, 3, 16, 39-48	
		Beckingham	42	
Newark District Council	86	Cranfield House	44-5, 48	
Newcastle Arms	89, 94	Dunham	45	
Newstead Abbey	18	Eaton	42	
NHS	86	Edgehill House	14, 42	
Norman Conquest	2, 39-40	Halloughton	42	
Normanton Prebend	39, 43, 47	Leverton	42	
North Muskham Prebend	42	Minster Lodge	42	
Norwell III Prebend	42	Normanton	39, 43, 47	
Norwell Overhall Prebend	42	North Muskham	42	
Norwell Palishall Prebend	42	Norwell III	42	
Norwood Park	5	Norwell Overhall	42	
Nottingham Trent University	109	Norwell Palishall	42	
		Oxton & Cropwell, Oxton II	42	
Oakum picking	81	Oxton I	44, 48	
Observations on Prison Discipline	74-5	Rampton	45, 47	
		Red	42	
Ofsted	37	Sacrista	39-40, 45	
Old Courthouse	65	South Muskham	9, 14, 42-3, 47	
Old Coach House PH	116	Woodborough	43-4	
Old Theatre	114-15	Pupil teachers	33	
Osmanthorpe	7			
Outdoor relief	77-9	Quakers	49	
Oxton & Cropwell, Oxton II Prebend	42	Racecourse	122	
Oxton I Prebend	44, 48	Rainbow Nightfreight	102	
		Rampton Prebend	45, 47	
Parliamentary Committee of Penitentiaries	71	Red Lion PH	89	
		Red Prebend	42	
Paupers	79, 81-2, 84-5	Reformation	16, 28	
Pauper framework knitters	119	Reindeer Inn	89, 94, 96-7	
		Restoration	42, 46, 48	

		Southwell R D C	3, 86
Roman and Saxon Southwell	7-14	Southwell Council Southwell Union	65
Roman bath house	8-9, 13, 22	Workhouse	54, 79
Roman drainage system	8, 11	Southwellian, The St Catherine's Well	32 121
Roman Empire	1, 7, 14		
Roman mosaic	1, 13, 22	St John's College	27
Roman pottery	10-11	St Mary Magdalen	
Roman villa	1, 8-10, 12-15, 23	School	27
Royal Horticultural Society	118	State Chamber	2, 24-5
		Temperance Movement	90
Sacrista Prebend	39-40, 45	Thomas Caunt & Co	101
Salisbury County Goal	72	Thurgarton Hundred	
Salvation Army	49	Workhouse	78-9
Saracen's Head Hotel	5-6, 42, 49, 89-93, 96-7, 99, 111-12	Toad Hall Treadwheels Turnpike	61, 65 73-4 3, 96
Saxon 'burh'	14		
Saxon cemetery	11-14	Wakefield Goal	72
Saxons	1, 7, 13-14	War Memorial	65, 112-13
Scottish Army	17, 29, 91-2	Warwick & Richardson	106
Secular Canons	39	Welfare State	86
Separate system	72	Wells	1, 2, 18, 118
Sherwood Foresters	5, 113	Wesleyan Church	49, 52-4, 56
Silent congregate system	72	Wesleyan School Westhorpe	33 118-20
Society for Prison Discipline	72	Westhorpe Hall Wheatsheaf PH	120-1 89, 94
Soke of Southwell	25	White Lion PH	89, 95
South Muskham Prebend	9, 14, 42-3, 47	White Swan Inn Workmen's Rest	87, 89, 94-5 119
South Well	2, 118	Woodborough Prebend	43-4
Southwell Brewing Co	98	Workhouse, Southwell	77-86
Southwell Community Archaeology	3	World War 1	22, 32, 64, 86, 101, 113, 122
Southwell Minster – see Minster		World War 2	32
Southwell Paddy	106	Worthing High School	32
		Y H A	64